SELLING SUNSHINE

Selling Sunshine

Surviving Teenage Motherhood,
Thriving in Luxury Real Estate,
and Finally Finding My Voice

MARY BONNET

HARPER
INFLUENCE

An Imprint of HarperCollinsPublishers

SELLING SUNSHINE. Copyright © 2024 by Mary Bonnet. All rights reserved. Printed in the United States of America. No part of this book may be used or reproduced in any manner whatsoever without written permission except in the case of brief quotations embodied in critical articles and reviews. For information, address HarperCollins Publishers, 195 Broadway, New York, NY 10007.

HarperCollins books may be purchased for educational, business, or sales promotional use. For information, please email the Special Markets Department at SPsales@harpercollins.com.

FIRST EDITION

Designed by Bonni Leon-Berman

Library of Congress Cataloging-in-Publication Data has been applied for.

ISBN 978-0-06-332780-1

24 25 26 27 28 LBC 5 4 3 2 1

For my husband, Romain,
my biggest cheerleader.
Thank you for the endless love
and support over
the past seven years.

For my son, Austin,
I'm so proud of the man
you've become. I owe so much of
who I am today to you.

CONTENTS

SELLING SUNSHINE

1

Oh Baby

"Oh my God. What am I going to do?" I turned to my best friend, Shelly, who was seated next to me in the driver's seat of her car, with what must have been a look of sheer panic. I was freaking out, and I couldn't hide it. I've never been particularly adept at concealing my feelings.

"Don't worry," she whispered, rubbing my arm reassuringly. "It's going to be okay." It was the right thing to say, even though it wasn't the truth. In her heart, she knew it, and so did I.

"I'm not so sure," I said, emotionally paralyzed, still gripping the positive pregnancy test I'd just taken, alone in a gas station bathroom, at only fifteen years old.

The moment I found out, I knew my life was going to change forever. Not just my present, but my future too. Suddenly, everything I'd envisioned for myself seemed uncertain. Would I keep the baby? And, if I did, would I be able to stay in school?

How would I manage that while taking care of a newborn? These types of questions flooded my mind as I tried to weigh my options about what to do next.

"We're going to come up with a plan," Shelly declared, nodding her head. I was grateful that she was trying to comfort me, but I could hear the apprehension in her voice.

"Oh my God," I repeated as I buried my face in my hands. "This can't be real."

"We'll figure it out. I promise." But she averted her eyes from mine. She was probably afraid that if she looked at me, I'd realize that her bravado was laced with doubt.

"How did this even happen?" I asked. It was a ridiculous, rhetorical question—I knew the answer.

My boyfriend Mike and I had been dating for a few months, and we'd had sex only a handful of times. Of course, I understood it takes only one time to get knocked up, but—clearly—that wasn't a compelling enough statistic to stop me. I actually remember one of my friends urging me to be careful, since I wasn't using protection. She warned me of the risk, which—despite my carelessness—I already knew to be true but ignored because I didn't have easy access to birth control. My parents were devout Catholics and didn't believe in premarital sex. And I was too young to have a driver's license or my own car. I was planning to ask my older sister, Sarah—who's three years my senior—to help me, but before I could do that, the writing was on the wall.

I realized instantly that I was pregnant. Not because I had any obvious symptoms. There was no nausea or exhaustion. No swollen boobs. I just felt it in my gut; it was an instinctual sensation that I couldn't ignore. Still, I had to confirm my suspicion with actual proof.

Thankfully, Shelly was able to drive and did have a car, so she got me my first test, which came out negative. You'd think that would have made me happy, but it didn't. Because I knew it was wrong. A few days later, Shelly took me to Hook's, a drugstore in Anderson, which is the main town on the outskirts of my hometown of Lapel, to buy a second test. And, from there, we went directly to the gas station down the street so I could pee on the stick in relative privacy. I couldn't very well take it at home and discard the evidence in our trash. What if my parents found it?!

As expected, the second test came out positive. I stood there, by myself in the bathroom, staring at the two solid lines that declared my fate. I was like a deer caught in the brightest head-lights, frozen and frightened, unable to retreat or advance. I squeezed my eyes shut and willed one of the lines to disappear. No such luck. My intuition had been spot-on, which was shock-ing and terrifying all at once. It's one thing to have a strong hunch. It's another to hold the verification in your hands, to see it in black and white—or in this case, pink—and to know that exactly what you'd dreaded had become a reality. I walked out of the gas station and climbed into Shelly's Chevy Cavalier, which was waiting for me in the parking lot.

"Try to calm down," Shelly urged. "Deep breaths."

I inhaled and exhaled, as she'd instructed, but nothing could ease the tightness in my chest or dissolve the lump in my throat.

Shelly offered a heartfelt smile, put her car in gear, and exited the gas station. We had snuck out to take the test after school, and we were able to go while not being supervised by either of our parents. She kept her eyes on the road as I sat silently, unable to find the words to describe the sheer panic that was pulsing through my veins. Fortunately, I didn't have to. My reticence spoke volumes, which Shelly heard loud and clear.

"You can't tell anyone. Not a single soul," I said, finally, more for my own benefit than for hers. I knew I could trust Shelly to keep my secret.

"I would never," she confirmed.

"Thank you." I smiled appreciatively. Certainly I knew I couldn't hide my pregnancy indefinitely, but I was also well aware that I needed a hot second to figure things out before it became public knowledge. And even before I told my mom and dad, which was the most daunting prospect of all—especially since my sister Sarah had gotten pregnant just six months earlier. The only difference was that Sarah was eighteen years old and away at college, which was slightly more palatable for everyone. She chose to keep her baby, a girl named Rebecca (who's now twenty-eight!). She also chose to drop out of college—engineering school in Ohio—to marry my brother-in-law, Steve, and have two more kids with him.

As Shelly drove me home, I compared my sister's situation to mine. Would it make telling my parents easier, because they'd already gone through the shock of my sister's pregnancy? Or would it make their reaction worse?

I stared out the window at the passersby going about their day, most likely without a positive pregnancy test to agonize over. I would have given anything to return to that state of normalcy. To have my greatest concerns be my upcoming math test and how much homework I'd have to endure that night. Things that had once seemed so important were suddenly frivolous by comparison.

Once we arrived at my house, I took another long, deep breath and then forced myself out of Shelly's car. I told myself

I had to bury my worries for the time being while I formulated a plan.

Easier said than done.

As I passed through the motions of my evening, the baby in my belly was all I could think about.

I was a cheerleader at the time, and the most pressing issue I had to deal with was our impending competition that weekend. It was a big one, and I couldn't back out of it a few days beforehand. If I did, I'd need a solid excuse, and divulging my situation to even one more person was simply not something I was prepared to do. Sure, I was nervous that a false move could hurt me or my baby, but I couldn't let my teammates down. Disappointing people is not in my DNA. I kept my head down and focused on school and the competition for the next few days. Luckily, we both made it through the competition unscathed and with my secret intact.

With this first challenge under my belt, I knew I had no choice but to figure out my next move. I'd already concluded that, in my case, an abortion wasn't an option. I understood that it would be the simplest solution. An easy "out," if you will. I'd had friends who'd had abortions, so it wasn't entirely taboo or even off-limits, but I just couldn't wrap my head around it. And it wasn't purely because I'd been raised in a staunchly Catholic household. I firmly believe that women should have a right to choose and that every circumstance is unique. All I can say is that I couldn't do it. I wanted to keep the baby.

This meant I had to confess to my parents. Above all, *that* was one of my ultimate fears, along with the crippling anxiety inherent in making the best decision for me and for my baby.

But before I shared the news with my mom and dad, I needed to tell Mike—the father. Honestly, I had no idea how he was going to react or how I was going to receive his reaction, one way or another. At the time, Mike was living at his friend's dad's house because of some unfortunate turmoil at home. His friend's dad owned a construction company, and I'll never forget pulling into his gravel driveway in Shelly's Chevy. There were a bunch of construction trucks parked in front of me, the house was on the right side and an office trailer on the left. Mike walked out of the trailer, and we stood beside Shelly's car, my stomach in knots as I summoned the strength to speak.

"So, I have something to tell you," I started, my voice quivering. If he noticed, he didn't say anything.

"What's up?" he asked casually.

"I'm pregnant." There was no reason to beat around the bush. I couldn't. I had to release the burden I'd been bearing for what felt like forever, even though it had been only a few days.

"Seriously?" His eyes widened, though his demeanor remained unruffled.

"Yes." I nodded.

"Uh, okay," he replied, wrinkling his brow. He was quiet for a moment as I shifted from one foot to the other anxiously. "Do you know what you're going to do?"

"I'm going to keep it," I answered definitively, searching his face for feedback.

"Okay," he said. One word. Nothing else. I couldn't tell if he was truly fine with it or if he was reeling internally, as I was.

Inherently, Mike wasn't a terrible guy, but he was young and reckless, and raised without much guidance, so he didn't have much of a chance. He treated me nicely most of the time, and he'd remained faithful up until that point. But his childhood hadn't been easy. His parents were divorced, his father was remarried, and Mike was raised in a very challenging house-hold, which meant he got into trouble often. He had a very complicated relationship with his dad and stepmom and had witnessed a lot of crazy shit. I remember seeing strange behavior as well, though Mike was often reticent to share anything too private or embarrassing. Mike idolized his dad, and they were very close. They mainly fought when his dad was drunk.

One time when I was at Mike's dad's house, his dad and stepmom had a bad fight. What was particularly odd about that incident was that, during their fight, his stepmom lost one of her large diamond earrings, and Mike's dad told me to get a metal detector. He said, "If you find it, you can keep it." I didn't want the earring, obviously, or anything to do with their argument, so I kept my mouth shut and waited for the moment to pass, as I was extremely uncomfortable. I also didn't want him to turn his anger on me.

I smiled nervously, unsure how to react.

He nodded and gave me a reassuring hug.

Even though I didn't really know where he stood, I was grate-ful that he handled the news pretty well and didn't make me feel any worse than I already did. In that conversation—and later ones—Mike never tried to push me toward abortion or adoption. He recognized, despite his own tumultuous situation, that it was my body and my choice.

The fact was, I couldn't hold the secret in much longer. I'm the worst liar ever, even if it was only a lie of omission. Typically, when I'm hiding something, everyone notices, because I look and act guilty. On some level, I assumed my parents already sensed that things weren't copacetic. Still, I was scared to death to tell them.

I waited a full week after confessing to Mike, until eventually I couldn't put it off for another day. I had already told my older sister, Sarah, and even though I don't remember the specifics of our conversation, I do recall that it was helpful to have her support, because she had just gone through the same situation. And my younger sister, Anna—who's two years younger than I am—knew as well. The proverbial elephant in the room was awkward for all of us. It was time to bite the bullet.

I remember pacing my bedroom and repeating to myself, "Mary, you have to do this. You *can* do this." I rehearsed exactly what to say and decided to go with something very simple, like "Mom and Dad, can I talk to you guys? I'm pregnant." I swear that was it! I knew it would be all I'd be able to get out. I was literally chanting it in my head as I walked down the stairs, through the dining room and kitchen, and up to the entryway of our sunroom at the back of the house.

When I got there, I opened the sunroom door slowly, to find them both watching TV. Under my breath, I counted to three and said exactly what I'd practiced.

"Mom and Dad, can I talk to you guys? I'm pregnant." Just like that. As soon as the words escaped my mouth, my stomach roiled, and my heart started pounding against my chest.

My mom, who was lying on the couch, shot up to a seated position and blurted, "What?!" Then she promptly lost her shit. "How could you do this and be so irresponsible?!" she screamed. "Did you not learn anything from what happened to your sister?"

My parents were still recovering from Sarah's bombshell when I dropped the same one, only so much worse, since I was just a sophomore in high school, and I had no interest in marrying Mike or raising a family together.

I stood in silence while my mom continued to carry on, hurling pointed questions at me, such as: *How could you have been so careless as to ruin your life in this way? What are you going to do now? How are you planning to take care of a baby while you're in school? How could you have been so stupid?*

The odd thing is that her anger didn't upset me that much. I'd anticipated it. And I understood it. It was when my dad stared at me blankly, tears pouring down his face, that I died a little inside. His intensely visible disappointment nearly tore me apart. I knew I'd broken his heart. And, in that moment, I started to cry too.

There was a big part of me that was relieved they finally knew. Concealing the secret was far worse than bearing the brunt of their anger and disappointment, but neither felt good. I was terrified that I'd completely messed up my life. I didn't know what to do. I was so scared and ashamed.

For a short while my parents did push me to give up the baby for adoption. My mom was much more vocal about it than my father was, but neither of them wanted me to "ruin" my life by becoming a teen mom. And as others began to find out—like the parents of kids at school—they weren't very kind about it. I had a huge scarlet letter emblazoned on my chest, which was mortifying for my family.

I can't pinpoint exactly why I was so adamant about keeping the baby. I've never considered myself to have a strong maternal instinct with kids. I do with my friends. I'm the first person to step in if one of them needs help or taking care of. I'm sort of a mother hen. But I don't love all babies in general. I'm not the person who wants to hold other people's newborns or coo over them. I've always been someone who's very focused on other things in life, like succeeding academically and professionally. But I stuck to my guns, despite my mother's strong opinion to the contrary. And, eventually, my parents accepted my decision, as long as I promised to stay in school, which wasn't even a question in my mind.

On March 26, 1997—during my junior year of high school—my son, Austin, was born.

I'll never forget that day. I was sitting on the sofa in the living room of our house with my younger sister, Anna, and our parents were in the sunroom. I suspected that I was in labor as soon as I felt the first contraction, but I was so frightened of what was to come that I didn't say anything to anyone.

After a few minutes, Anna looked over at me, saw the discomfort on my face, and the way I was shifting in my seat, and asked, "Mary, what's happening? Are you having the baby?"

"Oh, I don't know. I might be having some contractions," I said, trying to sound breezy. I thought there was a possibility they could be Braxton-Hicks, which are false labor pains, even though they were getting really close together.

"Mary, what are you doing? You need to go to the hospital right now!"

"I'm still okay," I insisted, gritting my teeth through the pain.

"Oh my God, Mary! Are you insane?" She stood up to try to encourage me to do the same. "You have to tell Mom and Dad and go."

"I hear you," I answered. "Just give me a few more minutes." I was terrified that I wasn't ready. It's one thing to have a baby in your belly and quite another to become a mother.

I called Mike, but he didn't answer. Finally, I went into the sunroom to alert my parents, and off we went to the hospital in Noblesville, Indiana, where my mom's friend was an obstetrics and gynecology nurse. Our families had been close for many years, so her presence was a big comfort for me.

Unfortunately, there was still no sign of Mike—it turned out he'd gone snowmobiling before he knew I was in labor. We were still dating, but just a month before I gave birth, I found out he had cheated on me. I didn't take it well and nearly broke it off with him, but I ultimately decided to forgive him. He made it to the hospital right before I gave birth.

We didn't know Austin was going to be a boy. If you can believe it, the doctors didn't do any ultrasounds on me, because I wasn't high risk. And I didn't push them to, because I was scared to death. Actually, they were pretty mean to me throughout the whole process. I assume it was because they were judging me for being so young and irresponsible. But, from the way I was carrying Austin—like a basketball, all out in front—everyone kept telling me he was going to be a boy, so that was my expectation all along. You couldn't even see that I was pregnant from the back. I wasn't spread out, which is apparently what happens when you're having a girl, or so people told me.

Regardless of my parents' initial anger, disappointment, and embarrassment, from the second Austin was born, everyone adored him, including me. I just had no idea what I was doing as a mother!

After the birth, I remained living in my parents' house while I homeschooled for the last three months of my junior year and for my entire senior year. I would go in to school to take tests, but that was it.

My mom and dad were very clear from the onset that they weren't going to take care of Austin so I could hang out with my friends. He was my responsibility from day one. With that said, my mother was great about teaching me what he needed and how to provide for him. She was very firm with me, because she wanted me to thrive and do it on my own.

She'd explain, "When he's up, you should be up. When he sleeps, you should sleep." I'll admit that she was riding my ass all the time! But I know it was out of love.

Without a doubt, there were many restless nights. I was exhausted all the time and really trying to figure things out. Thankfully, Austin was a well-behaved baby, so I never felt frustrated or resentful. It was just a lot to handle, especially at sixteen years old. Still, I never thought about dropping out of school. And I never took any kind of government support. I refused to be a statistic.

As for Mike, he was around, on and off. He came over for the first few months to visit and drop off little gifts, like mini Nike sneakers and cute outfits. He didn't spend a ton of time with Austin, or act in the accountable way a father would and should. But I was okay with that—he was making some really dumb decisions, including getting arrested multiple times for doing stupid shit, so I wasn't particularly eager to have him around the baby, especially without me or an adult I trusted there too.

I was working at Texas Roadhouse, where at age sixteen I started as a hostess, then eventually became a waiter. One day, while I was at work, I left Austin, who was just six months old, at Mike's family's home, where I trusted he'd be safe, thinking Mike wouldn't be there. I later learned that Mike ended up coming home and then spontaneously decided to grab Austin and take him for a "spin" in his truck. When I heard he had done that, given his history, it scared the crap out of me.

The last thing in the world I wanted was to keep Austin from his dad, but unfortunately, I just couldn't trust Mike to keep him safe. With my mother's guidance, I saw the importance of how big an impact these decisions could have on Austin's safety. And once that lightbulb went off, I had this feeling that unless I established some boundaries, something really bad was around the corner.

From then on, a new rule was established: Mike could visit Austin only under the supervision of my mother, who was extremely strict with him. She would write down what time he arrived and what time he left. If he was supposed to be there at 5:00 and he came at 5:03, she would document that he was three minutes late. It was a relief to know that my mom was so supportive of me. Unlike her, I was much more laid-back. As long as he was showing up for his son and making an effort, and either me or my mom could be there to make sure Austin was safe, that was fine. But I was wrong. When I was with Austin, and Mike would show up, he had a far greater interest in hanging out with me than he did with Austin. He'd come over to our house to see me and ignore his baby.

On more than one occasion my mom had to say to him, "Mike, this is your time with your son, not with Mary. You need to watch him, take care of him, and play with him."

Eventually, I'd make myself scarce during his visitations, hoping that my absence would force him to focus on Austin. But that tactic backfired, and Mike just stopped showing up altogether.

He kept taking me to court to try to gain some form of custody. He ended up screwing himself over because the judge would find out that he'd violated his probation from previous traffic offenses and also failed to pay child support that the court had ordered him to pay. So, sometimes, the judge would throw him in jail for a brief stint. The judge would also explain that Mike could see Austin as long as the visits remained supervised. But Mike wasn't cool with being overseen, which meant that—ultimately—I stopped hearing from him and was granted full custody of Austin. The court eventually revoked all of his parental rights.

I'd be lying if I said I wasn't relieved by the verdict. I knew without a shadow of a doubt that this was the right thing for Austin at that time. Mike had shown me time and time again that he did not want to be a devoted or responsible father. This made me believe Austin would not be safe under his care, and my job as a mom was to protect my son. We were both young and dumb, so I forgive him for not knowing what he truly missed out on. But it also made me incredibly sad. My heart broke for my son, knowing that his father would never be in his life. But this was really not my choice.

The first time this really hit me hard was when Austin was about three years old. One morning before preschool he woke up and started to cry.

In tears, he looked up at me and said, "I can't go to preschool today. Please don't make me."

"Why?" I asked. "What's wrong? Are you feeling sick?"

He shook his head and replied, "Because I don't have a daddy." It turned out it was Bring Your Father to School day, which, for obvious reasons, no one at the preschool had bothered to tell me. I was heartbroken, but I asked my dad to step in and he went as Austin's proud grandfather. It really does take a village!

I'm so grateful for my dad making that effort, but it didn't eliminate the absence of a true father in Austin's life.

*I*n the years following, Mike reached out less and less and, finally, not at all. Ultimately, he disappeared from our lives altogether. When Austin was nine, I got a random phone call from him—the first time I'd heard from him in eight years. I was surprised but not unhappy about it; I thought, and hoped for Austin's sake, that perhaps he'd matured and wanted to get to know Austin. I let him do the talking.

"Hey, what are you up to?" he said nonchalantly when I picked up the phone.

"Not much," I replied, eager to hear what his agenda was.

"What's new with you?" he continued as if no time had passed and nothing had changed.

"I'm just living my life in Los Angeles. I'm married to a great guy and taking care of Austin."

"Austin, huh." He paused, like he was unsure whom I was referring to. And then he said, "Oh shit, how is that kid?" *That kid?!* It was all I could do not to completely lose it at him. But I knew he wasn't worth it.

"He's fine, thank you," I responded, as evenly as I could.

"Cool. Do you like living in LA? What do you do out there?" he persisted.

15

I was speechless. I'm not sure why, since he'd been MIA for so long, but I was still in disbelief that he appeared to have zero interest in his child, and I wanted to get off the phone as quickly as possible.

"I've gotta go," I said, suddenly. Then I hung up and sat there in shock, allowing the magnitude of our conversation to set in.

Mike didn't care about Austin. He didn't think about him every day. He wasn't even a blip on his radar, which wasn't a crime, but it was a shame—for Austin, although more for Mike. He had no idea what an amazing son he had. That was his loss, even if he didn't realize it and never would.

I haven't heard from Mike since that day.

2

The Beginning

When I became a mother at sixteen, no one really saw it coming. Prior to getting pregnant, I hadn't had a lot of boyfriends, and even the ones I did have were more in name than in physical contact. Mike was the first guy I had sex with, and we had slept together only a handful of times before I got knocked up.

After watching my older sister, Sarah, have the same experience, I guess I shouldn't have been that surprised, but—again—she was older than I was. And, for my own part, I was always a good kid who played by the rules. If I could pick one word to describe my childhood, it would be *idyllic*.

From the day I was born, in Muncie, Indiana, on July 29, 1980, I was a happy baby. My mom says that, as an infant, I never needed more than five hours of sleep, which absolutely killed her. But, according to her, I wanted to be awake and alert, so as not to miss anything.

Apparently, I was so eager to get on with life that I skipped crawling altogether and started pulling myself up to standing so I could walk. Since I wasn't even one, I was slightly bow-legged, which most toddlers normally grow out of by around two. But to correct the way my knees curved outward, I had to wear leg braces like Forrest Gump for about a year. Of course, I didn't let those bother or hinder me. I'd still try to run all over the place and get into everything.

I also wore glasses as a kid. Thankfully, our neighbor Charlotte worked for an optometrist. At least once a week, my mom would have to take my glasses to Charlotte to be fixed, because I'd either fall asleep in them and bend them or crack them when I was messing around. In addition to the glasses and leg braces, I went to speech therapy, because I couldn't say the letter *R*. Fortunately, all three of these situations were resolved pretty quickly, and I was free to evolve into a tomboy throughout elementary school.

From kindergarten through sixth grade, I attended St. Ambrose, a small Catholic school in Anderson, Indiana, where we lived. Our classes had only about ten students in them, so you really had to follow the "letter of the law" and stay out of trouble, which I did—for the most part. There was one time when I got sent to the principal's office for yelling at the priest on the playground; he was trying to play kickball with the kids, but accidentally hit my younger sister in the head, and I went into big-sister mode, scolding him to be careful.

She called my parents in and said, "Mary Catherine isn't a horrible kid. She's got a very sweet soul. She's just . . . *spirited.*"

My mom replied, "That's a really good word for her."

The principal then added that sometimes, certain behaviors in children that adults tend to disapprove of become the things they are admired for in adulthood.

Sure enough, it's exactly who I am: an advocate for the people I love and things I am passionate about.

I guess I was somewhat rambunctious and always trying to figure things out. I had not only a lot of energy, but also a strong sense of right and wrong. If I ever did anything I felt guilty about, I would come home and punish myself even more than my parents would have punished me. I'd tell my mom everything I'd done wrong and what my self-imposed sentence was going to be.

I'd say, "I'm so sorry. I'll never do it again. I'm going straight to my room right now." And I would usually ground myself for much longer than my mom would've.

She'd grin and reply, "Okay, but don't you think you're being a little hard on yourself?"

And I'd shake my head and insist, "Oh, no, I deserve it."

I credit this discipline to my Catholic school experience.

The other kids in my neighborhood went to the public school, but we were still good friends and after school spent all of our time playing together. I lived on a dead-end street with about fourteen houses, and there was a lake at the end of the road. We would race around every evening and all day on the weekends, riding our bikes, roller-skating, and playing all sorts of games. It was exactly what you'd expect of life in the country in the Midwest. The only rule was that we had to head home once the streetlights came on. I'll never forget the summers of my youth, which were filled with sunshine, laughter, and unadulterated fun.

One of my best childhood friends, Lindsey, lived down the street from us. We used to call her Dennis the Menace, and although my mom adored her, she also drove my mom crazy at times. Lindsey had such a kind heart, but she was very rambunctious and was always causing trouble (the good old-fashioned kind). We used to leave the windows in our house open in the summers, while we were sleeping, and Lindsey would wake us up in the morning by standing outside my window and yelling, "Hey, Mary, are you awake yet? Come on, let's go play!" And then my mom would scream back, "Lindsey, go back to bed. It's not even six a.m. yet!" This was a daily occurrence. Reflecting on it now still makes me smile.

As I mentioned, I was a total tomboy. I loved climbing trees and catching tadpoles and frogs at the lake. I can't tell you how many times my dad would have to drop whatever he was doing and run out to scoop me up because I'd broken another bone. I'd be dashing about while flying a kite, and trip over a rock. Or I'd be pedaling my bike too quickly to get to one of my neighbors' houses and crash into something. I got hurt constantly, though it never bothered me.

The best part about growing up where I did was that our house had this amazing field behind it, where we created a massive fort (or at least it felt massive when I was younger). In my head, this fort—which I later realized was merely situated by this little patch of trees in the middle of the field—felt so far away, as if it were its own island. It actually wasn't much farther from our house than our neighbors' houses were. But that's the magic of childhood. Everything seems bigger and grander than it really is. Lindsey and I would take stuff out to that fort, like games and outdoor chairs, and blankets, all manner of things, and leave everything there like it was our home away from home. Sometimes, we'd make believe that we were runaways and the fort was our refuge. We had wild imaginations.

My dad also taught me and my sisters how to shoot BB guns in that field. He'd line up Coke cans, and we'd fire pellets at them, which we thought was super cool. He always made sure to make time for us. On Saturday mornings, my dad would take me and my sisters to get doughnuts, so my mom could sleep in. After doughnuts, he'd bring us to see the pigs and cows at this farm near the doughnut shop, which was one of my favorite things to do. With these trips, he would occasionally switch on and off between the three of us, from one week to another, so we'd each get alone time with daddy. My father has always been my hero. He may be soft-spoken and introspective, basically the polar opposite of my personality, yet we've always understood each other and maintained such a strong relationship. I have tremendous respect for him and know how lucky I am to have him.

Once my sisters and I were all in school, my mom decided to go back to college for her degree, and then for her master's—as my father had—so she could teach middle school English. To help support my mom's continuing education, my dad worked multiple jobs. On the weekends, he was a reserve in the National Guard, and the state historian, which was very cool. During the week, he was a high school history and geography teacher. After work, in the evenings, he would stock groceries at Pay Less, which is a chain of supermarkets in central Indiana. Looking back, I don't know how he juggled it all and still managed to carve out time to spend with his family.

One of my most vivid memories of that time is going with my mom to Ball State (where I went to college too). She was logging hours by helping a few students improve their reading skills as a requirement for her degree. We couldn't afford child-care, so if my sisters and I weren't in school and my dad was working, we would follow my mom around like little ducklings, doing what we still refer to as "The Ball State walk." We had these teeny tiny legs and would scamper behind my mom as she said, in her urgent voice, "You have to keep up!" And we'd hurry as fast as we could. Then we'd sit quietly in the classroom with her while she did her thing.

Even now, when I'm doing a photo shoot, and the camera person says, "Walk toward me," I literally take off in my highest heels. Without fail, they burst into laughter and say, "Oh my God, girl. This isn't an Olympic event. Slow down." I'm like, "I'm sorry! I was doing 'The Ball State walk,'" which is not at all graceful. Maybe I've still got a little of that tomboy in me!

Eventually, when I started middle school, I came into my feminine side a bit more, specifically as a cheerleader, but I also played volleyball and was still athletic. I was definitely in the popular crowd but never cliquey or nasty, like some of the other girls. I would try to be extra nice to everyone, especially the kids who got picked on for no reason. It's always been my instinct to help people and to lift people up when they're down. I could never understand why I was one of the lucky ones, who didn't have to endure the wrath of the mean girls. What made me special? Nothing. It simply wasn't fair, and somehow I knew that from a young age.

Right before my freshman year in high school, my parents were doing much better financially, and our family moved from Anderson to a big house in Lapel that my mom and dad designed and custom-built. It was deep in the country and didn't even have a paved street, just gravel, but it was a gorgeous home on a three-acre property, which we all loved. That was the year I met Shelly, who would quickly become my best friend and ultimately my confidante when I got pregnant.

Before the pregnancy, high school was a very happy time for me, even though my parents were pretty strict—less so my dad than my mom. She was the rule maker and the predominant disciplinarian, although she didn't always want to be. She admitted that to me many years later, and it made good sense, since my dad is typically a very passive person. With that said, in the rare circumstance when he does get mad, steer clear! You do not want to set him off, which takes a lot to do.

I will say that my dad was consistently protective of my mom, even when they weren't getting along. One of the few times I saw him really upset when we were kids was when my sister Anna disrespected our mother. I can't recall exactly what she did or said to my mom, but he flipped out. Anna was sitting on a barstool, and he swiped it right out from under her, and she fell on her ass. Then he looked her in the eyes and demanded, "Don't you ever disrespect your mother like that."

I remember thinking, *Oh, shit. I'm glad that's not me.* There was nothing worse than disappointing my dad, because he was so devoted to us and we all worshiped him.

But, again, those instances were few and far between. He really was a softy at heart. In high school, once my older sister, Sarah, could drive, we would cruise around this outdoor shopping area, which was the cool spot in town to hang out. We'd also go to this gas station—close to our high school, where my dad was a teacher—that everybody flocked to after school. We'd get burgers, pizza, and those monster-size Mountain Dews. Classy, right? My dad would say, "You're allowed to be there for thirty minutes and then come right back. Don't tell your mom."

Looking back, at that stage in my life, I thought that my mom and I didn't get along, but that wasn't really the case. She was simply trying to raise three girls with strong moral compasses and solid values. It wasn't that I misbehaved, it was more that I challenged everything and tried to think outside the box, conceptually speaking. My mom's perspective was: "This is what you have to do, so just do it." And I was like, "Why do I have to do it? It doesn't make sense."

I feel badly when I contemplate those moments, because she was and still is the most amazing mother and woman. While we may not have been extremely close when I was growing up, she was always there for me, and I'll never forget that. Over the last twenty years or so we have developed a very close relationship, and I couldn't be more grateful for her.

Unfortunately, throughout my high school years my parents began to fight a lot. I do wonder if Sarah's pregnancy and then my pregnancy made things worse for them, but I don't think they'd ever admit that. Honestly, I just wanted them to be happy. I remember thinking, *Why don't they get a divorce?* But we're Catholic, and that wasn't something people did as easily back then. My dad would try to avoid conflict, because he didn't want to engage, and my mom would fight for the relationship, which he took as attacking him; they're just two very different personalities. The only trivial bonus was that, whenever I heard them fighting, I'd take the opportunity to chat with a friend after-hours, when I typically wasn't allowed to be on the phone. Essentially, I took advantage of the situation, as teenagers often do when parents aren't paying attention!

Ultimately, my parents did get separated (and then divorced) as soon as Anna graduated from high school and when I was a sophomore in college, which was the best outcome for everyone, mostly them.

Overall, I have such fond memories of my childhood. To this day, my family and I will return to our former neighborhoods to stop into places like the little ice cream shop we used to go to and drive past our previous homes. We just like to see how things have changed and to reminisce. I'll never forget the first time I revisited that old fort in the field behind our house in Anderson and realized how small it was. As a child, playing there, I didn't understand how vast the world outside was or the endless opportunities my future held.

In my darkest times, I took refuge in these memories—my younger self had no idea about what was coming and the many obstacles I'd have to overcome to return to the happiness I once knew.

3

Moving On

"I'm on my way right now," I told my sister Anna as I hurried out of the hospital, juggling all of my stuff, with my cell phone sandwiched between my ear and my shoulder.

It was December 2000, my third year at Ball State University in Muncie, Indiana, and it had been another long day at school and work. I was totally exhausted, but I'd promised her I'd meet her in downtown Indianapolis for a meet and greet with LFO at our favorite radio station, WZPL, which was just a few minutes away from the hospital, and I'm always true to my word.

Anna was totally obsessed with LFO, a popular boy band, and she'd begged me to come with her. Since the concert was at a radio station in downtown Indianapolis, less than ten minutes from Methodist Hospital, where I worked, it was pretty easy for me.

"Are you okay?" Anna asked. I could tell that she was concerned about me.

"Yeah, why?" I replied, clearly distracted and tired.

At the time, I had an incredibly intense schedule. After graduating from high school in 1998, I'd started at Ball State that same year. Austin was only one year old, and we were still living at home in Lapel, Indiana, with my parents. While I was at Ball State, instead of pursuing a typical undergraduate degree, I'd enrolled in a special program with the intention of becoming a radiographer.

This line of work was very appealing to me, not only because it piqued my interest but also because it paid well. And radiographers were in high demand. As a single mom, I thought it would be the perfect career path to help support my little family of two for the foreseeable future. It would be a tiresomely intense schedule, but I knew I could complete it in less than four years. I attended classes during the summers, assumed an overload of classes every semester, and managed to graduate in only three years. Looking back, it was probably a bit too ambitious, but when I set my mind to something, I refuse to quit or even slow down.

I found the clinical training particularly fascinating because we did rotations in everything from pediatrics, fluoroscopy, surgery, and ER procedures to mammograms, CAT scans, and MRIs. But it wasn't easy. I had to learn all the different positions for the various machines and the necessary protocols, while also balancing my standard classes at Ball State—not to mention my obligations as a single mother.

When Anna graduated from high school in 2000 and my parents got divorced, my dad moved out. Austin and I then stayed with him. Eventually he began dating his current wife of about twenty years and would stay over at her house most nights, so Austin and I basically had his place to ourselves.

It was a great arrangement on the days when I didn't have to be at school or at the hospital until midmorning. This gave me plenty of time to get ready and drop Austin off at daycare. However, there were a few rotations that started super early in the morning, around 6:00 a.m., and my commute was an hour and a half, which meant daycare wasn't open yet. Thankfully, on those occasions, my dad was able to bring Austin to daycare for me.

After a full day of classes and clinical work, I'd pick Austin up from daycare and take him to Shelly's dad's house. His help was such an unbelievable gift. Shelly's dad loves kids and would babysit for me in the evenings so I could rush to my job at Texas Roadhouse. Without a doubt, I had an overflowing plate, which often consisted of a 4:00 a.m. wake-up call and a postmidnight bedtime—as there was still homework to be done once I got back from the steakhouse. I was physically drained and mentally fatigued around the clock. My friends and colleagues actually thought that I had narcolepsy because I could spontaneously fall asleep at any given moment.

The thing is: even when I'm at my peak stress level, if I have a mission, I have tunnel vision toward that goal. I tell myself and anyone who asks that I'm absolutely fine, and I'm going to accomplish whatever it is I'm striving for. I'm like the Energizer Bunny; I power through and just keep going and going until I hit a wall, same as when I was a kid. It's both a blessing and a curse, because on the one hand, it allows me to achieve success, but on the other hand, I push myself to an unhealthy point. And once I've finally run myself into the ground, my body will simply shut down, which means I'll get very sick and sleep for over twenty-four hours straight.

On the phone, Anna could tell I was more than just distracted. "You sound really stressed." She explained, "I know you, Mary. You're overdoing it, aren't you?"

"I'm fine," I maintained as I slipped into the driver's seat, preoccupied by my running late and the likelihood of traffic. I wasn't as big a fan of LFO as Anna was, but I still didn't want to be late.

Just an aside—the band ended up coming back to town a few months later for their concert, and we met them and hung out after the show. Brad Fischetti, one of the singers, and I really hit it off. A few days later we went to the movies with friends and Brad ended up driving us in my car and actually slightly damaging it by driving over something. But I didn't care, I was googly-eyed. One thing led to another, and before the band left town, Brad and I hooked up. He then invited Anna and me to their next gig, and we hung out a few times after that. He was a cool guy, very hot, but not serious at all. Though in my head, I'm sure I envisioned us running off into the sunset together. I was only twenty at the time and very naïve. It wasn't anything serious, but in my head, I was like, *Oh my God, I'm dating a famous musician!*

"Okay, whatever you say." Anna exhaled. "I'll see you soon."

"See you soon," I answered, before hanging up the phone and throwing it in my cup holder.

I turned on the ignition, shifted the car into gear, and took off. What I did not do was put on my seat belt—a reckless mistake that I would later regret.

As I cruised down the street, blasting music on the radio, I was feeling good, better than usual. Sure, my day had been hectic and demanding—and yes, I was still very tired—but I was also ready to let loose a little and tune out the noise in my head. I focused on the fun my sister and I were going to have together. We always did.

Maybe that's why I didn't see him coming when I crossed the intersection.

Without warning, another vehicle hurled down the road and T-boned me. Since I wasn't strapped in, I flew across the car and the right side of my body smashed into the passenger side door.

The next thing I remember is being in an ambulance, headed straight back to Methodist Hospital, where I'd just come from—an irony that was not lost on me.

At the hospital, I was in a tremendous amount of discomfort. The side of my body that had slammed into the door was throbbing. I have a high tolerance for pain, but it was excruciating. I remember nearly passing out from the sheer agony I felt when they lifted my arm for a scan. They didn't know what they were dealing with yet, and therefore, the clinician just kept trying to lift my arm to get the X-ray needed to treat my injuries. They had to give me morphine in order to get me through it, although that made me sick to my stomach, so they switched to a Demerol drip, which I could endure. It was brutal.

Once the doctor arrived to examine me, he told me I was going to be okay, because it was just my arm that was injured, but he said I was definitely going to need surgery.

He informed me that I'd shattered my right-side humerus. "That's the bone of the upper arm that forms joints at the shoulder and elbow," he explained matter-of-factly.

Obviously, as a radiologist, I knew what bone he was referring to, and that it wouldn't be a breezy recovery. "That doesn't sound great." I sighed. I was beyond disappointed in myself for failing to wear my seat belt. How could I have done something so blatantly irresponsible? I could have been killed.

"We can get you into surgery immediately," he stated plainly.

I had just finished a rotation with an orthopedic surgeon, Dr. Brown, who I knew was talented and thorough, so I asked if he could perform my surgery. I felt that if I wanted it done correctly, it should be executed by the best orthopod on staff.

But Dr. Brown was in high demand, and there were multiple level 1 trauma patients who were brought in by LifeLine helicopters, so I got bumped for surgery many times. For three days, in fact! The doctor told me it was a standard procedure, and I would be in good hands no matter what. Despite the constant and unspeakable pain in my arm, I told him I wanted to wait for Dr. Brown.

"It's your decision." The doctor shrugged and left me alone in my hospital room. I'm sure he thought I was being ridiculous or high-maintenance, but I didn't care.

As it turned out, my injury ended up being a spiral fracture with parts of the bone completely shattered. Dr. Brown had to insert a plate to hold everything in place and then use thirteen screws to piece my arm back together.

For the first few weeks after surgery, I wasn't allowed to lift anything heavier than a coffee cup, which was extremely challenging, given that I had a three-year-old child to take care of. Accordingly, I had to rely on my left arm and other body parts for everything—like using my knee to hoist Austin onto my hip in order to carry him around.

y February 2001, after only two months, I'd completely recovered. I was relieved to return to school and work. Plus, I was so ready to get back in the game. I'm not someone who enjoys sitting around, even if I'm sick or hurt.

But only three days after getting back to my regular schedule, my life was turned upside down all over again.

It was midnight, and I was just about to go to sleep after another long day at the hospital, when my phone rang.

"Hey, Mary!" Dave's inebriated voice reverberated through the line. Dave was a friend from elementary school. He was actually my first kiss. About two weeks earlier, we'd run into each other and reconnected after years of being out of touch. So, it was nice to hear from him, even though it was kind of late at night.

Unfortunately, Dave wasn't calling to just say hello.

He told me he had been celebrating his twenty-first birthday and had somehow gotten separated from the group he was with and lost his wallet. From the way he described the events of his night, I could tell he was pretty drunk. He said he was stuck in downtown Indianapolis and asked if I could come pick him up and drive him home.

It was the last thing I wanted to do. I was exhausted. I'd been going full speed since my first year at Ball State, completing required undergrad courses like anatomy, chemistry, and physiology. Then, in the second year, I'd devoted a couple of days to core classes on campus and spent the rest of the week doing full-time, hands-on clinical work at Methodist Hospital, which is a top-tier teaching institution. Now, in my third year, I was finishing up all of my requirements for both school and work, so I could graduate according to my self-imposed schedule.

"Dave, omg it's so late!" I replied, keenly aware of my own limitations. "I've been going nonstop all day, and I was just about to crash." A word I did not anticipate would become prophetic.

"Please, Mary. I don't know who else to call. I swear I'll make it up to you." He was slurring his words.

In addition to having a hard time saying no to people, I was somewhat concerned for his well-being, especially if he truly didn't have anyone else to reach out to. Also, my father was staying at the house that night and was able to watch Austin, which meant I didn't have that as an excuse. Thus, I relented, against my better judgment.

On the way to retrieve Dave, I felt wide awake. But by the time I'd picked him up and we were on the freeway heading home, my exhaustion kicked in. I could feel my eyelids getting heavy, so I rolled down my windows to let the fresh air in and turned on the radio to try to keep myself awake. With Nelly's "Ride Wit Me" blasting through my speakers and Dave passed out in the passenger seat, I kept driving, trying to stay alert.

I said to myself, *Mary, you will not fall asleep.* I repeated that mantra until, involuntarily, I started to nod off.

The last thing I recall was the sound of my Jeep rumbling over the rumble strip on the side of the road, which startled me to attention. Regrettably, my car was already angled toward a ditch on the perimeter of the freeway and there was a big sign right in front of me—I swerved to avoid it, and my tire got caught on a railing, flipping the car end over end. As we were overturning, my seat belt broke, the driver-side door was ripped off, and I was catapulted out of the car, onto the pavement of the highway.

To this day, I can remember that feeling of soaring through the air, although I don't have any memory of hitting the ground. I still have scars from the road rash all over my back and under my arm, which was also pierced beneath my armpit by a sharp piece of metal. When the police and paramedics arrived, I was unconscious, and they considered calling an emergency helicopter to transport me back to Methodist Hospital, but they decided to drive me directly there because I was right on the border of requiring that extra level of support.

Remarkably, Dave, who was out cold in the passenger seat, walked away from the accident. His only injury was a little chafing on the top of his bald head, from the ceiling of my car. The doctor later explained that, often, when someone is that drunk, they don't get injured as easily because their body is limp (as a result his seat belt stayed on). Whereas, when someone is sober, their instinct is to stiffen up and try to brace themselves, which isn't always the best approach.

Regrettably, I was not as lucky as Dave. I was unconscious for over twenty-four hours, had lacerated my spleen and liver, broken four ribs, and fractured my sacrum.

After I woke up and was stable, they wanted to take me into surgery for a splenectomy, to remove my spleen, because my blood levels were right on the precipice of needing it done. But I begged them not to unless it was 100 percent necessary. I literally pleaded with the doctor to give me a little while longer to see if my levels would improve. I explained that I'd just spent two months recovering from my first crash, and I couldn't take any more. Fortunately, my levels did get better within the day and he didn't have to operate.

Sadly, both of these accidents delayed my graduation for a few months, namely the second accident, since I had to go back on leave for about eight weeks.

I focused on my recovery, taking care of Austin, and then jumped back into my classes and work as soon as I could. Despite these major setbacks, I ended up graduating from college in late 2001 and taking a job at Community North Hospital in Castleton, Indiana, a suburb of Indianapolis, where I worked the night shift in the ER and performed CAT scans.

Unlike Methodist Hospital, which was nonstop action, Community North was very slow, and I was often bored. So much so that I would do crunches on the bed of the CAT scan machine during my downtime. As someone who likes to be challenged and feel inspired by my vocation, I realized pretty quickly that this job wasn't a good fit, and the experience nearly turned me off from a career in radiology.

Fortunately, even though I didn't love my job, there was a bright spot in my life. I started dating a great guy, a major league baseball player who'd been rostered with the New York Yankees and multiple other big-name teams. He also had a two-year-old son, which was one of the things that made us so compatible, and he was going through a divorce from his wife. He rented an apartment for the two of us in Castleton, on the outskirts of downtown Indy, so we could be together, even though he had to go home a lot to help with his son, which I really respected. He'd travel back and forth constantly, and I'm not sure how he pulled it off for the year and a half we were together. But we were happy, and I believed in him, so I didn't question it.

Then, the truth was revealed, and everything fell apart.

I wasn't able to attend one of his baseball games, so I watched it on TV from home.

He called me beforehand, and our conversation went something like this:

"Is your ex-wife bringing your son to see you play?" I asked.

"No," he replied, with certainty. "She can't make it because she's out of town."

"Oh, got it. Well, I'll be watching you on TV!"

"Thanks, babe. I'll talk to you later."

"Good luck!"

Once we'd hung up, I did exactly as I said and turned on the television. I guess I shouldn't have been shocked when, a few innings in, the cameraman flashed on the smiling faces of his wife and son. What's amazing is that I still tried to make an excuse for him by telling myself that maybe they'd arrived late as a surprise. Or perhaps they'd returned from out of town early. It seemed pretty unlikely, but possible, I supposed.

Once the game was over, he and I spoke for a second time.

During this conversation, I said, "How did it go? I didn't catch the end." Once I'd seen his wife and son, I'd turned the game off. "Did your ex-wife and son end up making it?"

"No," he responded. "I told you they're out of town."

"Right. Such a bummer. I know how much your son enjoys watching his dad play."

"Yeah, totally. Well, there will be plenty of other opportunities."

It was a blatant lie, and I knew then and there that I was done with him for good. I was so embarrassed that, even with the handful of red flags I'd ignored along the way, I'd allowed his dishonesty to prevail. I'd always been so supportive of his time with his son (and his wife), because I didn't think it was fair for me to act jealous when he was just trying to be an attentive father. I'd convinced myself that he was moving mountains to be with both of us because he was a decent man. But the truth is that I was an idiot. And our relationship was over. I refused to be the other woman.

I didn't think he deserved an explanation after this flagrant deceit, and since I was unhappy with my job as well, I decided to pull the trigger and move to Los Angeles, where I could start fresh. I chose LA because I wanted to move to a bigger city, but I hate cold weather. I also had a friend named Shannon who lived there, and I asked her if I could come check it out. At the time, I had no desire to be in the entertainment industry; I was focused on radiology and thought there would be great opportunities in LA.

Initially, I ignored all his voicemails, in which he said things like, "I'm worried. What's going on with you? Why are you avoiding me?"

Finally, I called him back and said, "I'm fine. I'm moving to California. We're done." As far as I know, he's still married to the same woman.

Even though the breakup hurt, I was ready to begin a new chapter in my life, in an exciting city I'd always wanted to live in. The plan was for me to leave Austin with my aunt and my mom while I got settled, secured a job, and found an apartment in an area with a strong public school. At that point, Austin

was five years old, and I couldn't afford private school or professional movers to transport my belongings to the West Coast.
So I drove my silver Mitsubishi with all of my stuff in it the two
thousand–plus miles from Indianapolis to LA.

*F*or the first time in my life, I was finally on my own. The
independence was exhilarating. My heart was still torn
in two after the breakup, and it was really hard to be away from
Austin, but I knew I needed to keep my head up. Luckily, LA
was the perfect distraction, especially since it's so drastically
different from Indiana. I was ready to get over my despair and
figure out a way to navigate my future.

When I first got there, I stayed at a friend's place in Studio
City. She was in Hawaii and another friend, Nancy, was living
there temporarily as well. Nancy and I ended up really hitting
it off and decided to find a new place together so we could share
rent, which was more expensive in LA than I'd expected. We
got a spacious two bedroom in Century City, and I finally felt
like things were coming together.

Astonishingly, two months later, out of the blue, Nancy—
who had broken off an engagement before we met and
had started dating our friend Edwin while we were living
together—came home and announced that she'd called
it quits with Edwin the previous night. She was engaged
again—I assumed to her former fiancé, though I never even
found out whom Nancy was engaged to. And she was moving
out immediately.

When she told me, I was shocked. "What the hell are you
talking about?! You just broke up with Edwin."

"I know. Isn't it great?" she replied, happily. "Now I'm finally going to be treated like the princess I am."

And that was that. She'd already packed up all her things, so she just walked out the door, never to be heard from again, leaving me in the lurch with a two-bedroom apartment I couldn't afford by myself. Unfortunately, I was responsible for the entire rent, as is standard in California for co-tenants and even for co-signers on any financial application/lease. This is why it's important to choose your roommates and co-applicants wisely.

At the time, I was working a per diem job in radiology at a hospital in Valencia. Not only was it an hour away from my apartment, but my shifts were at night, which I knew would present an issue when Austin came out to live with me. It also wasn't the position I'd hoped for, and I was being paid barely enough to cover the gas for my commute.

When I originally relocated to LA, I was under the impression that hospitals were offering signing bonuses for radiology techs, which they had been. But after one of the hospitals was shut down for issues about the building's safety, all of the techs who'd been working there filled the jobs that were open elsewhere in the city. To make matters worse, the hospital I was at was reminiscent of Community North—very quiet and uneventful. Honestly, it felt like torture to report to work every day. Not to mention that I was broke.

Right before I truly ran out of cash, I managed to get a job as a loan processor from a friend of a friend. I had no experience, and it certainly wasn't glamorous, but seeing as my bank account was practically empty, I was willing to take whatever was offered to me. I still had to scrounge together the funds to pay for my two-bedroom apartment and to take care of Austin. Even though he was staying with my aunt and mom, I was covering his expenses too.

It was a very stressful period for me, and I had to fight to keep my head above water. Losing a roommate and a friend was a setback, but—after the better part of a year living in LA—I was grateful for the community I was starting to build and was determined to make it work. I made an effort to meet people and invest in friendships with whatever extra time I had.

One of those new friends was Amanza Smith—who is now a costar of mine on *Selling Sunset*.

Surprisingly, our paths first crossed when we were living in Indiana, where we both grew up, but we didn't realize it until we were reintroduced in LA. I'd been invited to a party shortly after I'd arrived, and when I showed up at the door of the apartment building—which coincidentally is directly across the street from the current location of The Oppenheim Group—Amanza and her friend Andy were standing there, also waiting to be buzzed up. Amanza and I now have matching tattoos of those exact coordinates!

We shared a smile, as if we vaguely recognized each other, but it wasn't until we got upstairs and were out on the balcony that I broached the subject.

I said, "You look so familiar to me. Do I know you?"

She laughed and replied, "You've probably seen me on television, or maybe on a billboard." I couldn't tell if she was being serious or not, but I knew that wasn't it.

We still joke about that moment, because Amanza wanted to be a model back then, so whenever we talk about it, we'll laugh and I'll say: "I guess you're still waiting on those headshots!"

Amanza and I kept chatting and trying to figure out how we were connected. Finally, it hit me that we had a mutual friend from Indiana.

I asked, "Do you know Eric Anderson?"

"Oh my God! Yes!" she exclaimed. "He's my ex-boyfriend."

Eric used to show me pictures of Amanza all the time, so her face was ingrained in my memory. Shortly after I met Amanza, I also discovered that she was in my personal photos from an Indy 500 event I was at when I was casually dating a race car driver named Tomas Scheckter. He'd invited me to attend the race and then accompany him to the VIP events afterward. Amanza was also there with her boyfriend at the time, JC Chasez from NSYNC, and we started chatting at the events. I had a distinct recollection of these funky rainbow-colored leg warmers she was wearing, because I thought she had a really cool style. Apparently, we then took a few snapshots together, which is so strange to think about, given that she's now one of my closest friends.

After Amanza and I reconnected at that party in LA, we promised never to lose touch again. Ultimately, we decided to live together. Amanza was supposed to have her own apartment, but it fell through and she was staying with a friend. Since I'd just lost my roommate to a random engagement and was hoping to rent the second bedroom so I could afford to remain living there, Amanza asked if she and her friend could move in temporarily. Neither of them were making any money, and they couldn't pay rent, but I allowed it anyway. Again, I have a really hard time saying no to people, especially when they need help. Unfortunately, supporting Amanza and her friend only further delayed Austin coming to live with me.

I wasn't proud of having left him with my mom and aunt for so long, but I knew that I was following my long-term plan, which was to create a better life for me and Austin. I wasn't willing to go on welfare or live in a trailer. I really did have the best intentions, but I felt a lot of guilt and shame surrounding the circumstances. I was embarrassed I wasn't able to stick to my original timeline. But the scene in LA has a way of making everyone think about themselves—and if I'm being honest, a big part of me also relished the freedom.

Between having very strict parents and getting pregnant at fifteen, up until moving to LA, I had never done anything exciting or been able to just do exactly what I wanted. During my first few months in LA, I probably went a little overboard with the partying, yet—simultaneously—I never stopped working my ass off. I was burning the candle at both ends, personally and professionally, which isn't always the best combination.

Finally, after a full year on my own, I called my mother to let her know that I was ready for Austin to join me in LA. Austin was about to start kindergarten, which was a milestone I didn't want to be absent for, and I missed him so much. I was flying back and forth to see him all the time, but it wasn't enough, and we'd been apart for too long.

I was definitely nervous because I didn't have everything set up for us. I didn't have my own place, and I wasn't as stable financially as I wanted to be. I had to break my lease to save money in the long run and lost quite a bit of money in the short term. I just knew that I had a responsibility as a mother and couldn't let this situation go on any longer. I didn't want to be the kind of person who gives up on her child and takes the easy way out.

Additionally, even though my mom had undoubtedly enjoyed her special time with her grandson, I knew it would be liberating for her to relinquish her responsibilities. She also strongly believed that Austin should be with his mother and felt it would be best for all of us for him to live with me in LA.

She knew I had a lot on my plate—as per usual—and asked me if I was absolutely sure I could handle it. I reassured her that I could, hoping to imbue similar confidence in myself.

My mom understood how much I'd sacrificed to make it work in LA, and to get myself to a place where I was ready for Austin to come live with me. She told me she loved me and that I was doing the right thing.

I thanked my mom for everything she'd done for me, and for Austin, but there was nothing I could really say or do to show her how grateful I was for her support. I decided the best way to demonstrate my appreciation was to step up for Austin and create the best life I could—to try to become the kind of mom she was to me.

After just a few short weeks, Austin finally moved to LA, right in time for summer, and I was so happy to be with him. I felt whole again. At first, we lived with Amanza in her friend Andy's apartment, in order to save money. The apartment had enough room for the four of us, and we were hanging out together often anyway.

I didn't know Andy super well before moving in to his apartment with Amanza, but very quickly I realized there was a spark. Andy and I started dating, and our romantic relationship accelerated fast. By the end of the summer, Andy, Austin, and I moved again—to our own place in Santa Monica in a great school district.

Andy was a cool guy and really kind to Austin, though he had barely any involvement with him, which was my choice. I never wanted anyone I was dating to feel or act like Austin's father unless they were prepared to be a real father figure, which I didn't believe Andy was, even though I liked him a lot.

But things that burn bright, often burn fast. And this was the case with Andy. He ended up being not a great guy and getting involved in all kinds of stuff I didn't want myself or Austin to be involved with. So, Andy and I parted ways after about eight months in Santa Monica.

Even though breakups are never easy—believe me, I've had my fair share—one positive thing that came from my liaison with Andy is that I met my first husband, Jeff, who was a friend of his and often came over and hung out with us. Jeff was a highly successful lawyer whose marriage was on the rocks, and he'd confide in me about his devastating divorce. After Andy and I split, Jeff rented a place in Hermosa Beach, and Amanza, Austin, and I stayed with him so we could help comfort him while he nursed his broken heart.

Though we'd known each other for only a few months, I really enjoyed Jeff's company and admired his dedication to his family. He had two sons, who were around the same age as Austin, and all the kids would play together. It never crossed my mind that anything romantic would evolve between us. He was about fifteen years older than I was and, before his divorce, had been madly in love with his wife.

Around 2004, after I'd been staying with Jeff for about a month, he approached me and asked how I would feel if he got us two apartments side by side in Redondo Beach, right on the water. I was shocked, and flattered, by his suggestion—it sounded amazing, but I wasn't quite sure what was in it for him. Our relationship was still completely platonic.

Jeff explained that living all the way downtown, by his law firm, was too far away from his old house, where his ex-wife and children still lived. Plus, Austin and his kids got along so well, and the property he was looking at seemed perfect.

It made sense, but I was also keenly aware of how generous his offer was.

Jeff knew I was struggling financially, and he was doing very well for himself. He understood that allowing me and Austin to stay in one of the apartments would be not only a huge help but also super convenient, because our kids could then play together. It was the first sense of normalcy I'd experienced in what felt like forever. Eventually, we even opened up the walls between the two spaces to create one massive apartment, with just a door in between. It was a beautiful situation, where two completely platonic friends were supporting each other in multiple ways.

Then, about six months into our friendship, our relationship turned into something more. Jeff and I had been out for dinner and drinks, which was a normal occurrence for us—sometimes we'd go out just the two of us, sometimes with our kids, and sometimes with other friends. That night, after we returned home, Jeff kissed me for the first time ever, in the doorway of our apartment, where one of the bedrooms and the living room met.

I was so surprised, but I certainly wasn't upset about it. I truly had no idea he felt that strongly for me, and I didn't know until that moment that I had romantic feelings for him. Jeff was just this unbelievably charismatic person. Everyone who

knew him understood that he was such a force and such a beautiful, caring, protective human being. In the beginning, it was
simply a friendship where, when the world felt so unsafe and
out of control, there was this man who was the kindest, most
devoted, most intelligent person who swooped in like a knight
in shining armor. And, ultimately, my affection and admiration
for him, and my gratitude for everything he'd done for me, for
Austin, and for all my friends, turned into something more. I
fell in love with him.

From there, we moved back into Jeff's old house in Palos
Verdes, since his divorce had been finalized. And, in 2006, he
sold the house and we rented a place a couple of doors down
so the kids could stay in the same school. During all these
changes, there was a two-year stint when I wasn't working. I
helped take care of Jeff's kids and was able to spend quality
time with Austin. For the first time, I was actually able to be a
fully present mom. Austin always had a lot of friends, though
he was a very quiet kid. He wasn't really into sports at this
age, but I encouraged him to be involved in at least one sport,
which turned out to be soccer. Nearly every weekend, it was
like pulling teeth to get him dressed and to his game, but we
did it for a few years. I was also very involved in his classes and
at his school. These years were really a special period of my life.

In 2007, we relocated to Hermosa Beach, got married, and
I started studying for my real estate license. Jeff had a lot of
wealthy friends, and I figured they could introduce me to clients
who were looking to buy or sell a home. It felt like the perfect
career for me to pursue while also attending to the kids.

Unfortunately, about a year into our marriage, Jeff's health
took a turn. As a teenager, he had been diagnosed with

achalasia, a rare swallowing disorder where the esophagus muscles don't contract properly and don't help propel food down toward the stomach. At one point, before we were married, he had to have his esophagus removed and replaced with a portion of his colon, which created a lot of health issues, including pneumonia; it was really tough. All the time I'd known him, his illness had been under control, but suddenly, his health started to spiral. As a result of a number of circumstances I won't share out of respect for him, I simply couldn't watch him deteriorate any longer.

Jeff was strong, but these struggles changed him and our relationship in a way that neither of us could control. And it simply didn't make sense for us to be together any longer. In 2009, with acute grief, we terminated our marriage, and a couple of years later he passed away.

I will always cherish Jeff for the wonderful person he was, for all that he did for me and for Austin, and for the amazing legacy he left behind. I truly believe he's still watching out for me from the other side. Even though he's gone, he'll never be forgotten. May he rest in peace.

4

When It Rains, It Pours

After Jeff and I divorced, I wasn't in a great headspace. I thought I'd finally found my person, and I was devastated when it didn't work out. Austin was eleven years old, in sixth grade, and we moved in to a small apartment in Hermosa Beach, so I could keep him in the same school and try to maintain some level of normalcy for him and for myself.

Because of the 2008 financial crisis, the year following was a tough time in real estate, and I had to support myself and Austin. Thankfully, I was able to get a job at Shorewood Realtors, which was also in Hermosa Beach.

Despite the divorce, and the challenge of working in real estate during this recession, I loved living in California. I was slowly getting accustomed to my new life as a single mom when, a couple of months postsplit with Jeff, I met Drew. I didn't think I was ready to date someone new yet, but I was still capable of recognizing a hot guy when I saw one. And, apparently, so was the clerk at the Kinko's across the street from my office, where I'd stopped in to create some marketing materials for an open house I was selling.

"Well, he was yummy." The clerk smirked at me, referring to the handsome British man who'd just exited the store.

"Yes, he was." I blushed, regretting that I hadn't made eye contact with him before he left.

When I first noticed Drew, he was pacing back and forth by the copy machine while yelling at someone on the telephone. Perhaps that should have been an indication to steer clear, but he was so good-looking, and his British accent made him even more attractive.

Once he'd left the store, I walked outside to head back to my office, and Drew was still out there. He'd ended his call, and when he spotted me, he immediately struck up a conversation.

"I'm Drew," he said, with a beguiling smile.

"Mary." I smiled back. If nothing else, it felt nice to be noticed.

"Good to meet you, Mary." I liked the way he said my name.

"Good to meet you as well," I replied self-consciously. I've always been excruciatingly awkward in these types of situations.

"Can I interest you in grabbing a coffee?" he asked.

I thought he was pretty forward for a perfect stranger, but not in a bad way. Minus his angry phone call a few minutes earlier, he seemed like a nice-enough guy.

"Oh, thank you so much, but I'm actually married," I said, instinctually. Hot or not, I really wasn't prepared to get involved with another guy yet.

"I see." Drew nodded and narrowed his eyes at me.

It was almost like he knew I was lying, but if he did, he didn't say as much. And, just like that, we went our separate ways.

A few weeks later, I was still reflecting on our encounter and kind of beating myself up for turning him down. I thought, *Maybe I should get back out there. I deserve to find love a second time around.* In that moment, I promised myself that if I ever ran into Drew again, I'd let him take me out. Then I quickly shook the notion from my mind, as the possibility of encountering him twice seemed highly unlikely.

That was where I was wrong.

In a surprisingly providential turn of events, the following day I was in my car stopped at a red light in Redondo Beach, and I looked over to find Drew sitting in the car right next to mine.

I was like, holy shit! Did I manifest his reappearance?

As soon as he saw me, he grinned and said, "Well, how do you like that. Now can I get your number?"

I was so flustered that I said, "No, sorry."

"Where are you going?" He ignored my rebuff.

"An open house," I replied.

"Who do you work for?" he asked, eager to keep me engaged.

"Shorewood Realtors."

"Got it." He winked, and the light turned green.

"I've got to go." I waved and took off.

I've always been a bad flirt—I don't know why it makes me so uncomfortable, but it just does. I chastised myself for what was probably my last missed opportunity. And I doubted I'd bump into him a third time.

To my true astonishment, as I parked in the driveway of the open house, my phone rang. An unidentifiable number flashed on the screen. I figured it was a prospective buyer, so I picked up.

"Hi. This is Drew." It was a male voice, with a British accent. "The guy from Kinko's and the stoplight."

I was so shocked that I responded, "How the hell did you get my number?"

"Sorry, I didn't mean to startle you." He spoke kindly. "You said your name is Mary and that you work for Shorewood Realtors, so I looked you up on their website and found your picture and contact info."

"Oh, that makes sense," I said, appreciative of his effort.

"How about that coffee?" He was nothing if not persistent.

"Let's do it," I agreed. It felt like kismet, and I wasn't about to let him slip away again.

Drew and I started dating shortly thereafter, and I learned that he had a one-year-old son. He also shared with me that he grew up in Romford, which is a large town in East London. Later, he became a trader in London and then moved to Miami to pursue real estate, which is where he met his son's mom and she got pregnant. When their son was about six months old, his son's mom got an offer to pose for *Playboy*, so they relocated to LA, and eventually, Drew became a single dad. That's one of the things that endeared me to him in the beginning. I thought he had to be a good guy because he stepped up and took care of his son, whom he clearly loved very much.

Once in LA, Drew became business partners with a lovely, older man, who was also British and was a general contractor. They had a stucco company together and ended up branching out to do subcontractor jobs. Drew also got his general contractor license, even though he didn't actually do the work himself.

*A*bout a year after we met at Kinko's, Drew proposed. We were engaged for six months, and then got married at a gorgeous cathedral in Indiana—where I'd wanted to get married ever since I was a little girl. I was madly in love with Drew, and my heart was full as we said our vows—with Drew's toddler son clinging to my leg and calling me Mom—in front of family and friends, including many of Drew's, who had traveled from the United Kingdom to be with him on this day. It was a truly magical time. Or so I thought.

While I danced and chatted with guests from near and far, I was blissfully unaware of the ill-fated drama unfolding in the next room. I was still oblivious on the following day when Drew and I embarked on our honeymoon—a Mediterranean cruise with stops in southern Spain, the south of France, Italy, Croatia, and Montenegro.

But about two days into the trip my mom called me with startling news.

"Hey, honey," she began, sounding graver than I'd expected. "How's your cruise? Is everything going okay?"

"It's great, thanks," I answered tentatively. Why wouldn't it be?

"Right, well, I just want to let you know that I'm going to be forwarding you a bill for the damages from the wedding venue." She cleared her throat.

"Damages?" I asked, confused by her insinuation. "What are you talking about?"

"Oh, you know, broken wineglasses and stains on the wall."

I still had no idea what she was talking about. She went on to explain that Drew and his mom got into a massive fight during the reception and started throwing wine at each other, breaking glasses against the walls.

I was in complete disbelief. "You saw it?"

"Yes, honey. I think everybody saw it."

But I didn't. I couldn't wrap my head around what she was telling me. How could I have missed that? Once we'd hung up, I went directly back to our cabin to confront Drew.

I swung the door open, marched right up to him, and said, "What did you do to our wedding venue? And how come I'm just hearing about this now?"

Unruffled by my accusation, he replied calmly, "My mother had one job, which was to hold on to her grandson during the ceremony, and she couldn't even do that, so I was very upset with her."

"And then what?" My hands were on my hips. I was going to need a better explanation than that. "How did it go south so quickly?"

"Then she screamed at me, and we got into it. It really wasn't a big deal." He shrugged, as if it happened all the time. Did it?

"It is a big deal. You did a lot of damage, and now we have to pay for it. My mom is sending us the bill."

I was aggravated not only by his carelessness but also because he didn't seem the least bit fazed by his actions.

It made me think about our wedding night when, after the reception, we went back to our hotel and Drew wanted to go to the bar before heading to our room. I was still in my huge wedding dress and just wanted to change into something more comfortable and spend the rest of the night alone with my new husband. But he insisted on "one more drink," and I relented. Then he got drunk and spilled red wine all over my white gown.

When I saw the crimson-colored stain, I shrieked, "Oh my God!"

In turn, Drew simply looked at it and laughed. He didn't care at all, and he was too inebriated to do anything about it.

I remember the bartender looking at me and saying, "I'm going to help you. Hang on." He was trying to make it better because he saw the horror on my face and realized that Drew's indifference was very peculiar. A minute later, he returned with stain remover. "This is definitely not meant to be used on a wedding dress, but it's probably your only hope."

I smiled and replied, "Thank you so much." I was grateful that someone—certainly *not* my new husband—gave a shit.

Of course the stain didn't come out completely. When we got up to the room, I expected Drew to apologize, but instead he passed out immediately.

I was like, *Well, this is super fun. Guess we're not having sex on our wedding night.* And, of course, the next day when we went to the airport to leave for our honeymoon, he was completely hungover. It was a total nightmare, and I completely brushed it to the side.

There were other warning signs I should have noticed, but in the beginning, it never seemed like they were aimed at me. I'd hear or see something that wasn't right, and I'd think, *That doesn't seem normal.* Occasionally I'd confront Drew about a specific situation, and his answer would make sense, although

I would have handled whatever it was very differently. Then there were other times when I'd be so disgusted by something he did, and I'd speak up. I'd tell him I wasn't going to fix his mistake and then he'd get really mad.

The most striking example of this was when he'd take someone off a construction job for whatever reason and then they'd say he didn't pay them. I'd try to explain to him that he couldn't do that. I'd tell him that they did the work and he had to compensate them for it. I wanted to impress upon him that these people had families; they had to put food on the table. They were literally living paycheck to paycheck. They could have their electricity shut off. I'd been in that situation myself. Whether it was true or not that he'd reneged on their pay, it seemed to me that Drew's moral compass was incredibly different from mine, which should have been a red flag that he could eventually screw me over too.

It wasn't always easy with Drew, to say the least, but eventually, we settled into our life and even ended up working together. I'd been building my real estate career at Shorewood, and he'd started his own construction company. I was at open houses every Sunday, and with two young kids between us, the hours we spent working and our different schedules were becoming an obstacle. Since the construction company was making a lot of money, I decided to put real estate aside and join him. My job title was office manager, since I was much better at business and managing money than he was. His whole system was chaotic, and I realized that being in a relationship with Drew was like being married to Dr. Jekyll and Mr. Hyde—you never knew which personality you were going to get.

To make matters more complicated, while we were trying to grow the business, we decided to get pregnant. Unfortunately, we had trouble conceiving the natural way, so we had to resort to IVF. I think he was a little discouraged by the clinical nature of it all, but I didn't mind.

As luck would have it, I got pregnant with twin girls after our first round of IVF. At this point, I relished being a hands-on mom for Austin and Drew's son, and I was ready to have more kids—way more ready than I was the first time around! For one, I wasn't a teenager, and also we weren't strapped for money, so it made everything go so much more smoothly. Drew was fully on board. Or at least that's what he told me.

Sadly, at around five weeks, the doctor informed us that one of the babies had stopped developing, and that there was no longer a heartbeat. It wasn't the news I'd hoped to hear, but I tried to take it in stride. I was still excited that there was another healthy baby growing inside of me, and it was so early on.

Then, eleven weeks in, I was on a field trip with Drew's son at a pumpkin patch and my stomach started cramping, which led to bleeding. I couldn't leave the field trip, since I was a chaperone, so I called Drew, but he wasn't picking up his phone. I was trying not to freak out, although, in my gut, I knew I was having a miscarriage. With no word from Drew, I went home after the field trip, made the kids dinner, helped them with their homework, and then went directly to the doctor, where my suspicion was confirmed. I'd lost the second baby, and I had to endure the physical process that accompanied that, which was heartbreaking.

A couple of days later, after dropping the boys off at school, I was still feeling really down, so I went home and crawled into bed.

Drew came into our room, stood over me, and asked, "What are you doing?"

I looked up at him, exhausted, and replied, "I'm just resting."

Without warning, he went ballistic. He screamed something like "Oh, this is how it's going to be now?! Grow the fuck up, Mary! It's over, so stop crying and moping about it."

My eyes stung with the threat of tears as I explained, "I literally just had a miscarriage. My body is still going through the healing process."

It wasn't as if six months had gone by, and I was still dwelling on it—and even then, that would have been okay if I needed more time to recover. But only two days had passed, and his reaction was so over-the-top and aggressive. I truly didn't understand what was going on.

He added that I was the one who had wanted more kids. And therefore what happened wasn't his fault; it was mine.

I was so confused, because that simply wasn't the case. I said, "You wanted more kids too. What are you talking about?"

He responded quickly and decisively that he hadn't and he'd said he wanted kids only because I did.

Defeated, I said, "Well then, I guess you're in luck, because the babies are gone." And that was that. The subject was dropped.

A couple of months went by before the loss of our babies came up again.

Drew didn't want to talk about it, but the subject was the elephant in the room. In turn, I didn't want to struggle with my feelings alone, and I didn't think it was healthy for us to just pretend it hadn't happened. So I ignored Drew's resistance and finally forced a conversation, during which he got angrier and angrier with me—I could tell he was ready to explode. It was a crazy fight, and things very quickly escalated to a scary level.

In the aftermath, I was in shock. I called my sister Anna (who was already living in California) and asked her to come over. I was still shaking when she arrived, in disbelief that my relationship had reached this point. I told her everything—the awful fight we'd had about the miscarriage, how unsafe and alone I felt with this man it seemed I no longer even knew. As always, my sister was there for me. She didn't criticize me or blame me for not catching warning signs about Drew earlier, and she didn't make me feel ashamed that my husband was clearly not the person I thought he was.

Austin and I ended up going home with Anna that day, and then I stayed with her for at least a few more days. Honestly, I don't even remember how long. That was the beginning of a long period where I would leave Drew and go back to him. He would apologize to my mom and to my sister but, at the same time, ask me not to tell them everything. He'd argue that since we were trying to work things out, it was better that they not know everything. But I do remember that I ran back to my mom and my sister on quite a few occasions, even though I never shared the full truth with my mother.

After that explosive fight and my brief respite with Anna, Drew tried to move forward and resolve things. Miraculously, he even apologized to me. I wanted to move forward too—I was exhausted, and a big part of me desperately wanted somehow to return to the happy, loving man I'd met. But a bigger part of me also knew that something had been irrevocably broken. Even after everything blew over and things between Drew and me seemed okay, I recognized this moment as my first clear sign that my husband wasn't the man I'd thought he was. And that realization made me deeply sad.

Before this fight, I knew he had a hard time regulating his emotions—his mom even insinuated he had a bad temper. Stupidly, I'd blamed her insinuations on their tumultuous relationship and didn't think I'd ever see that dark side of him.

Although Drew did admit, albeit rarely, that how he treated me wasn't right, I don't believe that he ever completely grasped why what he did was wrong. He always came up with some justification for his actions, whether it was that he'd had too much to drink or he was stressed-out. He'd say he felt badly and tell me that I had to forgive him, otherwise I was being unreasonable. That was his mindset most of the time. I'd usually say something like, "I need to sit on this and see if you can prove to me that you can be stable." The high highs and low lows became too much for me. He'd pretend to acknowledge what had happened, and then five minutes later he'd go berserk all over again. And I was like: I guess I have my answer. When I look back on this period in my life, I truly can't believe I stayed with him. I was so ensconced in the relationship that it was as if I were brainwashed.

There were definitely moments when I'd get really upset and put my foot down, and then after a couple of days, I'd be like, I just can't be bothered to be angry anymore, so I'd let it go. I hate drama and negativity around me. It drives me crazy.

The sad thing is that I loved Drew so much, which made it that much more confusing. When he was good, he was really good; he was my best friend. But then he would have these episodes, and it would be as if a switch flipped inside his brain. He would go from being my best friend to being a nightmare. Nothing made sense; I couldn't do anything right. Sometimes I'd stand up for myself, but then if the fight dragged on, I'd say, screw it, and forgive him. Although I never forgot. And I never will.

I will admit that at one point things got better between us for a while. Our construction business continued to thrive, and there were fewer altercations between us. I was anxious about our future but wanted to keep the peace for our children, and for myself. Things weren't perfect, but I was hopeful that maybe our big fight had been merely a weird fluke.

But about six months after that big fight, the shit hit the fan. Two big projects arose that ended up landing us in major debt. The first was not Drew's fault—a subcontractor who didn't pay us—which we could have recovered from. It was the second project failure that did us in.

Drew wanted to take on a major hotel as a client. He insisted that this was the deal we needed to bounce back from the money we'd lost from the subcontractor. He wanted to go big and was sure that we would make a lot of money.

But I didn't agree. The risk of something going wrong was too great—if this deal failed, then we would be completely screwed. I told him I didn't think we had the bandwidth to do it successfully, and that I had a bad feeling about it.

Naturally, Drew didn't listen to me. And, as I'd predicted, that job took our company down. When the deal didn't work out, it launched a domino effect, which required us to come out of pocket with a ton of cash that we didn't have. In a last-ditch attempt to remain afloat, we ended up dipping into our personal savings to pay all of our workers, but it was no use. Unfortunately, I was the guarantor on everything for the company, because I had perfect credit, a circumstance that—in retrospect—was not an intelligent move on my part.

As the company continued to disintegrate, Drew didn't handle the tremendous amount of stress well, and it took a major toll on our relationship. Should I have considered divorcing him then? The simple answer is yes. However, life isn't simple. At least mine hasn't been. More than anything, I wanted to hold our family together for the sake of my son. His own father had never been in his life. My first husband, Jeff, who'd been his father figure, was in the past. So I desperately wanted to fix things with Drew, which against my better judgment I thought I could do.

Therapy did help in the beginning. But with the stress from our struggling business and then Drew's dad getting cancer, therapy wasn't nearly enough. Something had to give.

In light of this, we decided to make a fresh start and move to London, where Drew's father was living, so we could be closer to him while he was sick. I recall being very excited about the move for multiple reasons. For one, everything in our life was going downhill, and I thought that relocating to a new environment might improve our situation. I've always loved traveling overseas and learning about various cultures. I understand that for most people a change of that magnitude might have seemed scary, but for me—especially since things were not going well in our current situation—it felt like a smart resolution. I'm not going to lie; it was taxing to sell all of our stuff on a wing and a prayer, though I didn't see another way to make things work, which I really wanted to do.

Also, once we found out that Drew's dad was ill, that seemed like a compelling reason to be near him as a show of support. Drew had never been particularly tight with his father, and my hope was that our transfer to London would improve their relationship. I'd met his dad only a handful of times and knew very little about him. I did know he'd been raised in a very rough, violent neighborhood, and, probably for that reason, he wasn't the warmest person. But he was always lovely to me. I often wondered what he would think of his own son's nasty behavior, but I never mentioned a word of it to him.

I had enough self-awareness to realize that I wasn't perfect either. I could be confrontational and antagonizing at times. I told myself that I was probably pushing Drew's buttons much of the time. I thought, maybe if I didn't poke the bear, the bear wouldn't lose his shit.

Obviously, I was in serious denial and willing to try anything to make the marriage work. I just wanted to move forward as a happy family.

Austin and I were mostly on the same page about moving to London. He didn't know what to expect but still found it ex-hilarating. Despite that, he was much more nervous than I was. I just thought it was going to be a fresh start for us, not only professionally but also in terms of my relationship with Drew. It was hard to say goodbye to my friends and family. I knew that I was going to miss them and have to meet new people in a completely foreign city, but I also thought it would be a welcome diversion to relocate to a fun new place.

When we first went over, I took Austin to Paris on the Eurostar; we took one of those red double-decker buses and saw all the sights. I wanted him to truly experience Europe and all the amazing culture it had to offer. I think traveling is such an important part of being a well-rounded, well-educated person.

When we first moved to London, we lived in Brentwood, which is a town in the county of Essex, in the east of England. Drew had a friend who had just gotten divorced and owned this huge, beautiful, old English home, with five bedrooms. It was built in the 1700s and had this very narrow staircase; you had to be super careful walking up and down it. Drew's friend was such a nice guy, a real family man. And he let us stay with him, since we didn't have a place of our own yet. His mom, dad, and sister would come over frequently.

Of course, we couldn't live with him forever, so after a couple of months, we relocated to Chislehurst, a suburban district of southeast London, in the Borough of Bromley. We found a great school for Austin in Chislehurst; it was called Coopers, and he liked it for the most part. All of the kids thought he was so cool, since we'd come from LA.

But since we'd moved in November, and the British school calendar is different from that of the United States, he was about six months behind everyone in his grade. So he was constantly trying to play catch-up, while not only attempting to learn this whole new educational system and curriculum but also adjusting to this new environment. Austin had always prided himself on being smart and feeling ahead of his classmates academically, so this change was challenging for him.

Austin also missed the company of Drew's son, even though he was only five or six at the time. His mother, Drew's ex, had reentered her son's life and wouldn't let us take him overseas, which made sense. By that point, she'd married someone and wanted her son back in her new life and family. She'd gotten her act together and ended up being a phenomenal mother. Still, Drew didn't like her, so I was the one who communicated with her. She and I got along great, in part because I understood that she was young when she got pregnant and I felt that if she'd turned things around and wanted to be active in her son's life, she should have that opportunity.

Unfortunately, as much as I loved living in London, things didn't improve between me and Drew. I quickly started realizing that I'd gotten myself into a bad situation. Not only did Drew not change—I'm not sure why I expected he would—but he also controlled all of my finances. I'd literally have to beg him for money to cover basic expenses, like groceries.

Then there was one particular day—which I'll never forget—when the shit really hit the fan. Drew told me he was going to a work lunch at noon and that he'd be home around six o'clock. I thought that seemed like an awfully long lunch, but I didn't make a big deal of it. Before I knew it, it was nine o'clock at night and there was no sign of him. I emailed him to ask if he was okay and what was going on. I got no reply. I emailed him again at 11:00 p.m. and, as with two hours earlier, nothing. Finally, after midnight, he got back to me, saying that he was hopping in a cab and coming home. I was like, "What the hell have you been doing? You went to lunch and it's over twelve hours later. This makes no sense." He claimed that he went out for drinks after. I was furious. By 3:00 a.m., he still wasn't home. Then, it was 6:00 a.m., and no Drew. He didn't return until 8:00 a.m. I was like, "Fuck you! I can't believe you're doing this." And his nonchalant reply was that I needed to stop worrying and that this behavior was normal for people in London. I said, "What are you talking about?! People in London say they're in a cab coming home and don't appear until eight hours later? That's absolutely ridiculous."

It wasn't so much that I was suspicious about what he was doing; I just thought it was rude and disrespectful. I was yelling at him: "What is wrong with you? I gave up everything for you to move here! I expected a fresh start and now this?!"

Sadly, that was just the beginning. Everything went drastically downhill after that.

Don't get me wrong, we had our good days where we'd get along beautifully. He could be very tender. And, when that was the case, it felt like I'd married my best friend. But then, unexpectedly, he'd transform into a total asshole. It was a vicious cycle that was too much to bear.

As I said, our relocation also, temporarily, gave Drew complete control over our finances. This infused him with a false sense of power. He told me that when you have only a spousal visa, as I did, you're not allowed to have your own bank account, so all of the money we'd accumulated from selling our house and everything in it had to be transmitted to him. I believed him, even though, in retrospect, I'm not sure if that was actually true. Regardless, what it meant was that I didn't have access to any of our money, which was a nightmare. It also meant that I was at his mercy in a whole new way. I couldn't even get a job when we first arrived there.

Thankfully, after about a month or so, once I got my visa, I got a job at The Crown Estate, which is one of the largest landowners in the UK—they own and manage land to benefit the nation, sitting between the public and private sectors. When I started working there, I was just a receptionist. I would greet everybody who came in to see the higher-ups—people who were there to petition for things, to sign deals, and to meet with the various heads of departments. I really enjoyed my time there. It was very posh. All of the female employees had to dress exactly the same—in black silk shirts, black pencil skirts, black tights, and black heels; everything was completely uniform. Also, our hair had to be pulled back and wrapped around these doughnut things to make the perfect bun. At first I thought it was a little weird, but I got used to it, and it made getting ready in the morning very easy. It was a peaceful job that I got paid for, which afforded me a little financial freedom from Drew.

Still, things were very rocky in our relationship. The only other good news was that Drew's dad ended up going into remission after about a year or so after we moved there. I then decided to take Austin to visit my mom, who was living in Arizona. We both needed a break from Drew.

What I didn't anticipate was Austin's feelings about returning to London with me, especially since he was only fifteen years old.

As we were nearing the end of our respite, he came to me and said softly, almost under his breath, "Mom, I don't want to go back with you. Please don't make me."

"What did you say?" I asked, confused and somewhat wounded by the words I was sure I'd understood.

"I said, please don't make me go back to London with you." He looked down at the ground, to avoid making eye contact. I could tell it wasn't easy for him to share his feelings with me.

"Austin, you have to come back with me. I'm your mother. We can't live apart from each other." I shook my head to indicate my position.

"Please, Mom," he pleaded. "Let me stay here and finish high school in Arizona."

On the one hand, I couldn't believe what I was hearing. In one respect, I was insulted that he didn't want to be with me, and it broke my heart to think that we'd be separated by over five thousand miles. But on the other hand, I knew that Austin craved stability, which I couldn't give him while I was still with Drew. Austin recognized that my marriage to Drew was toxic, and it was overwhelming him.

"I have to think about it," I said, reluctantly.

Then our eyes met and he said, firmly but sweetly, "I can't go with you."

In that moment, I knew I had to respect his wishes. I thought about staying in Arizona with him, but I felt like I had to return to London and figure out what was going to happen with my life there. I should have done things differently, but I couldn't change the facts. Austin was old enough to know what he wanted, and he never complained about anything or asked me for anything more than I could give, so when he begged to remain in Arizona with my mom, I couldn't say no. I also knew it was the best way to keep him safe and that

I couldn't let my ego or my emotions stand in the way of his well-being.

"Okay," I relented. "But I'm going to FaceTime you every single day."

"Thank you, Mom!" He hugged me tightly, and I didn't know whether to burst into tears or beam with pride. My baby had grown into a self-assured young man.

With that settled, I returned to the UK by myself. Drew and I moved again, this time from Kent to Central London. At this point, Drew had lost his previous job and was also looking for work, which meant that, in addition to my position at The Crown Estate, I had to work nights as a bottle service girl, which is the same as a cocktail waitress but typically at more expensive establishments. At that time, I would have taken almost any position. It wasn't anything special but it kept me busy, brought in more money, and was also only a ten-minute walk from where we were living. I'd leave The Crown Estate, start at the bar/club at around 7:00 p.m., and stay until about one or two in the morning. I hated it. It was very different from bartending because there was no physical bar to create a barrier between me and the men, so they could grope me, which really creeped me out. I was like, I'm here to serve you drinks, make some extra cash, and then I'm out. I didn't want these strange men touching my back, grabbing my hand, or whispering in my ear. I tried to be nice because I needed the income, but I didn't like it one bit. And Drew didn't appreciate it either. He would come pick me up and see these guys talking to me and freak out. Of course that didn't help our relationship either.

Thankfully, eventually I got poached by a man named Nick Candy, who's a British luxury property developer. This new job paid significantly more and allowed me to stop serving cocktails. We met when Nick came into The Crown Estate to talk to one of the heads of development. He was impressed with me and wanted me to work for him, so he had his headhunter reach out to me. Fortunately, the job with Nick also allowed me to fly back to Arizona and visit Austin. When I returned to London after that visit, Drew had, to my surprise, moved out of our rental apartment, and—since things were so bad between us—I got my own place, a simple room rental within the home of a lovely woman, which was similar to living in a hostel. Drew didn't want me to leave him and he pleaded with me to come back to him, but I said no. And that was when things really went from bad to worse.

The final straw was when I found out Drew had cheated on me and I confronted him about it. We had a massive fight that night at his apartment in Canary Wharf, which is in East London. He was sharing it with another guy, who was from Turkey, but his roommate traveled frequently and was out of town. When the fight escalated past the point of my comfort, I managed to run out of his flat, albeit without money or my phone. I'm not sure why, after everything that had gone down between us, this was what finally compelled me to leave him for good, but it was. And it may very well have been the best decision I've ever made.

After hours of wandering the streets aimlessly, I ended up at Angel train station—a London Underground station in the Angel area of the London Borough of Islington—sitting on a bench, weeping, and trying to figure out what the hell I was going to do and where the hell I was going to go.

By the grace of God, amid my distress, a saintly stranger approached me and allowed me to use his phone. Even today, I don't remember anything else about that night or about this person. I just recall him coming up to me and his kindness. I called Anna—the only number I knew by heart. She was also the only person who had an inkling of what Drew had put me through. When things had gotten really bad between us in LA, it was Anna I went to for help.

"Hello?" Anna answered on the first ring, which was a relief, given that she didn't recognize the number.

"It's me. Mary," I said, trying to hold it together for her sake and mine.

"What's wrong?" She knew instantly, probably by the tremor in my voice, that I wasn't okay. Not even close. She'd been down this road with me before. "Where are you calling me from?" She sounded concerned, which made me even more emotional.

"The train station in London. This man let me borrow his phone," I explained as tears streamed down my cheeks.

"Mary, tell me what's going on." Her concern had morphed into alarm.

"Anna, I can't go back to him. I have to get to Arizona."

"Oh my God, Mary. I'm so sorry. We're going to get you home. What can I do? I'm worried about you."

"I know you are. But I'm going to be okay. I'm never going back to him."

"Okay," she said, warily. She had more questions, about how I would get home and how I would communicate without a phone, and I did my best to assure her that I'd figure it out.

"I'll find a way," I said. I knew Anna didn't have enough money to pay for a flight overseas, and I had barely a dime to my name. I couldn't ask my parents without telling them how bad things had gotten with Drew. They had no idea, and I planned to keep it that way for as long as possible—maybe forever.

"I don't love this, but all I care about is that you're safe. Please be safe, Mary."

"I will."

"I love you."

"I love you too."

It's crazy, but I don't even remember who ended up buying my ticket home or most of how I actually got home to Arizona. The experience was so awful that I blocked a lot of it out.

I do remember that it was around the holidays, and Austin was elated when I told him I'd be with him on Christmas morning. We didn't speak about why I was there or why I wasn't returning to London. I kept that close to the vest, mainly because I knew that the details would be too much for anyone in my family to endure. Everyone was just overjoyed to have me back where I belonged.

Although that was hardly my happy ending. A few days later, when I tried to lease a car, I was promptly denied. I was so confused—I didn't have much money, but I had perfect credit. Or so I thought. It turned out that Drew had gone online and applied for and received multiple credit cards in my name, because he had all of my personal information, including my Social Security number.

He'd amassed a whopping debt, running up the bills like we had cash to burn.

I had to file for bankruptcy. More important than figuring out my financial situation, I also had to explain to Austin that I never should have allowed Drew to treat me poorly and take advantage of me. I should have walked away immediately and given up on saving our family. I told my son that it was something I'd regret forever.

I then knew I had to pick up the pieces of my life—of our lives—and focus on becoming the woman and mom I wanted to be.

5

New York State of Mind

With my family around me and my marriage to Drew mostly behind me, I felt a massive amount of relief. But it was also scary. I knew I had to set things up for myself in Scottsdale and tell everyone that I wasn't going back to London, so there would be no way I could change my mind. I didn't want to be in limbo anymore. I needed to move on, and in order to do that, I had to formulate a plan. This meant I had to figure out where I was going to live and find a job.

As it happened, Anna was home for Christmas too, and she was unhappy in LA; she'd just gone through a breakup and had decided it would be the perfect opportunity to move to Scottsdale, so we could spend more time together. So I flew out to LA with her to help pack her things and drive her Jeep back to Arizona.

Fortunately, we ended up getting a cute two-bedroom town house with a little patio outside that was just five minutes from where our mom and Austin lived. It was the perfect scenario. I was able to see my son every day, and sometimes he'd sleep over at our apartment, yet he didn't have to compromise the level of his education, since my mom resided in a better school district.

Meanwhile I sent my résumé to a bunch of different plastic surgeons' offices so I could take care of my bills and keep my head above water while I mapped out what I wanted to do next. I was no longer licensed in radiology, since licenses expire after a certain amount of time. I was interested in plastic surgery, though I did look into real estate too, but I needed something that was going to pay immediately.

I was fortunate to land a job working as a receptionist for Dr. Bomer, who specialized in cosmetic procedures and whose office was located not far from our apartment. She was, and still is, well-known in the industry, and it was a very positive environment, which was exactly what I needed after the mess with Drew.

But just as I was beginning to settle into my new life, my past reared its ugly head, in the form of another phone call from Drew.

"Mary, I know you're upset about how things played out while you were in London, but you have to come back. We can make this work," Drew appealed.

It wasn't the first time he'd called, but I'd ignored all of the others. I had no interest in speaking to him or hearing what he had to say. I was well aware that no good could come of it.

Eventually, however, I realized that if I wanted him to grant me a divorce and maybe recoup some of the money he'd stolen from me, I couldn't avoid him forever.

"Drew, I'm sorry; that's not going to happen. I'm happy where I am," I clarified. Though I actually wasn't sorry at all. I'd finally come to understand that nothing that had transpired between us was my fault, even if I had pushed his buttons on occasion. Just the sound of his voice evoked memories of our final violent fight and made me sick to my stomach. I couldn't subject myself to that level of post-traumatic stress anymore.

"Mary, this is ridiculous. We love each other. You can't just leave someone without warning and never return," Drew pressed.

"I needed some distance." I tried to keep my answers simple. I knew that the more I engaged with Drew, the more he'd try to draw information out of me and convince me to get back together with him.

Also, I didn't want him to be able to find me.

"You've had distance. Now you need to be in London with me so we can figure things out. *Together*." I detected the irritation in his voice.

"Again, Drew, that's not happening. I want a divorce. You know why."

I still hadn't divulged to anyone but Anna, not even to our parents, that he'd mistreated me. I knew it would have killed them, but I'm sure many people close to me had their suspicions. And I definitely didn't say anything to Austin, even though I'm sure he knew some of it from when we all lived together. I told myself that what was done was done. There was no sense in dredging it up or continuing to discuss it. Honestly, I didn't want to think about Drew or give him any more attention than he deserved, which in my estimation was zero.

"Please don't say that, Mary. You know I love you. We're so great together. Just the two of us." His tone was softer now, almost solicitous.

There was no doubt that Drew was a smooth talker, which made it hard to resist his overtures. And, despite everything, I still loved him. On the one hand, I wished that things could be different between us. But, on the other hand, I said to myself: *What the hell are you thinking? Why would you ever consider putting yourself through that agony again?*

I always believe I can change someone—it's a dangerous Achilles' heel. For this reason, I knew I had to cut ties with him altogether. I simply couldn't allow my mind to go there.

Not to mention that he never said he was sorry or even acknowledged what he'd done to me—at least not at the time. Many years later, I received some random text messages from him apologizing for his actions, but no amount of regret on his part could justify his behavior or alleviate the pain he'd inflicted on me. It was too little, too late.

"Drew, I have to go," I stated, bluntly. I had to extract myself from the conversation before he convinced me to do something I definitely didn't want to do, which was to give him another chance.

"Wait, Mary—" he implored.

I hung up before he could say another word. I'd heard quite enough.

After we spoke, Drew refused to grant me a divorce, and I never saw a cent of the money that he'd taken. I hated being tied to him in any way, even if only by a piece of paper, but I had no choice, so I let things remain as they were for the time being. After years of feeling like someone else was dominating me, I focused on taking control of my life. I ended up going a little overboard—in an attempt to empower myself and reclaim my future—by relying heavily on structure. My life became very regimented, down to the littlest things.

For example, I typically sleep on my stomach, curled up against a pillow, but the doctor I was working for had informed me that sleeping on my back at a specific angle was better for warding off wrinkles on my face, so I slept at that exact angle every single night, religiously. I began eating extremely health-fully, exercising daily, and sticking to a stringent schedule. I went to bed early each night and woke up early each morning. I started going to hot yoga—in the middle of the summer in Arizona, which was scorching. I was also super tight with my finances. Since Drew had bankrupted me, I had to kick my ass into gear in order to save money. I was willing to do whatever it took to set my life back on the right course, as long as it was good for me and for Austin.

About six months later, Austin graduated from high school and got accepted to the University of Arizona. He'd looked at a bunch of different schools: UC Santa Barbara, UC San Diego, and the University of Florida, which were all out of state and so would have been too expensive. He also looked at Northern Arizona University, and Arizona State University—which was a real party school, though I never worried about Austin in that respect. I actually wanted him to go to Arizona State, since it was closer to home, but he ended up picking the University of Arizona because they had a department of biochemistry, which was what he wanted to study. It was such a proud moment for me and for our family. I couldn't believe that, at only thirty-four years old, I had a son who was going off to college.

Thankfully, he was able to get some financial aid, but I had to pay for the rest of it myself, which wasn't easy. I wasn't making a lot of money, and things were very tight. Every time a bill arrived, I was like, *Oh my God, how am I going to do this?*

Just before Austin started college in August 2014, I made the decision to leave Arizona and move to New York. I was excited and ready to explore a city I'd never lived in before and, also, to meet new people and explore new places. It felt like the perfect fresh start (again). I sent my résumé to a bunch of different medspas and plastic surgeons' offices and ended up landing a manager position at a celebrity facial spa. I'd always wanted to live in Manhattan, and it seemed like an amazing opportunity at just the right moment. For the first time in my life, I had no day-to-day responsibilities for anyone other than myself, so I decided to take the plunge.

Living in New York was going to be insanely expensive, even more so than Los Angeles, and definitely more than Scottsdale. Thanks to Drew, my credit was no longer great, which would make it impossible to qualify for an apartment on my own. Still, I wasn't put off by that. I moved to the Big Apple and started searching for a cheap Airbnb or a place on Craigslist. While I looked, I stayed in a hostel with all of my belongings, desperate to save the little money I had left and to make sure I had enough to cover Austin's tuition bills.

Each day, I would leave the hostel with my enormous suitcases and drag them with me on the subway and all around the city. If I'd left my belongings at the hostel, it would have cost an extra thirty dollars for the night. I told myself that if I found an apartment that day, it would be a waste of money. Looking back, that was completely crazy, as you can very rarely move in to a new apartment the day you find it! But at the time, I was determined—even if it meant doing things the hard way, I would make my new life work.

About two weeks later, Anna also moved to New York. I was thrilled, since it meant we could find a place together. I would have my sister by my side, and we would be able to split the rent. I was still in the hostel when she arrived, and I'll never forget her reaction when she walked through the door to meet me there.

"Mary, are you kidding me?" She looked at me like I was an absolute lunatic.

"What?" I feigned ignorance, even though I knew exactly what she was going to say.

"This place is *disgusting*. What the hell are you doing here?" Standing in the doorway, she took in my dingy surroundings. Obviously, I realized it wasn't a palace, but I didn't really have much of a choice, and I've always been someone who can endure whatever it takes to remain afloat.

"It's not that bad," I insisted.

"Yes, it is. It's awful. We're getting out of here right now. Come on." She waved me in her direction.

"Where are we going? We don't have anywhere else to sleep. Let's just stay here until we can land an apartment we can afford."

"Okay, you're crazier than I thought. We're checking in to

a hotel for a few nights. Pronto." Her hands were on her hips now. She wasn't kidding.

"Do you have any idea how much a hotel room costs? I'm not going to pay for that, not even for one night," I lamented.

"It's my treat. I'm not taking no for an answer."

I relented, only because I was enticed by the prospect of getting out of the hostel, enjoying a hot shower, and sleeping in a bed with clean sheets.

And that's precisely what we did.

Immediately after that, Anna got a job working for celebrity dermatologist Dr. Lisa Airan, which paid decent money, and we were able to find a dirt-cheap apartment, which we believed was on the Upper West Side but was actually in Harlem. Still, it was a major upgrade from the hostel—we thought we were living the life. We shared the place with this big, muscular guy, whom we called A. He looked like a football player, although he worked at a bank, and he was super sweet to us. Anna and I had one room, without a bed, and slept on an air mattress together on the floor for a couple of months with our two Chihuahuas, Niko and Nína. The funny—or maybe not so funny—thing was that A had this massive cat, which was probably the width of my body and came up to my waist. At night, the cat would creep into our room while we were sleeping and claw the hell out of our air mattress. Every morning, we'd wake up with it partially deflated, lying at an angle on top of one another, and we'd have to tape up all of the holes and blow it back up.

After living in the Harlem apartment for about three months, with the city blanketed in a thin layer of snow, Anna and I moved to Alphabet City, in the East Village of Manhattan, where we stayed in this really cute Airbnb studio apartment that was so small, all it had was a tiny kitchenette, an even tinier bathroom, and a bedroom that could fit only a full-size bed with hardly any space to walk around it. When Anna's boyfriend slept over, it was the three of us in the bed together, which—in retrospect—is both hysterical and ridiculous.

They'd have to go into the bathroom when they wanted to have sex—but with such a small apartment, there wasn't much privacy, and I'd be sitting there on the other side of the door! Anna and I still laugh about the time she and her boyfriend accidentally broke the bathroom sink and water started squirting everywhere.

Fortunately, we lived in that place for only eight months before finding a bigger place in Williamsburg, a neighborhood in Brooklyn, which we thought was going to be fabulous. How wrong we were! It turned out there was black mold in the bathroom, and when we told the landlord, she didn't seem to care. She said, "We'll try to send someone to look at it," but she never actually did.

For a while, we couldn't use our shower, and when we had to use the toilet, we'd hold our breath. It was insane. On top of that, everything in this apartment was constantly breaking, to the point where I would come home from work and find parts of the ceiling falling in.

Yet, somehow, Anna and I didn't let it bother us. We were so grateful for the little things and to have a roof over our heads, even if it wasn't exactly stable.

Apartment woes aside, things were going reasonably well, but I still had a few concerns.

Number one was that Austin had been telling me he was happy in college, but I could tell from our phone calls that something might be up. Eventually, after a lot of pressing, he admitted to me that with all the distractions in school it was hard for him to concentrate on his studies. Initially, he was very quiet about it, even though I was always asking him how things were going. I suggested that if he felt the University of Arizona was too much for him, maybe a community college would be a better choice. If he wasn't able to focus, and especially if he wasn't going to be forthcoming about his issues, I couldn't keep paying that much money. I tried to explain this to him—and hopefully motivate him—by saying things like "If you're not studying, and you're not passing exams, and you can't thrive in this environment, why am I paying for it?" And, "If you won't tell me the truth, you're not going to succeed. I'm throwing money away."

He eventually decided to complete his course requirements by taking summer classes and then switch to a community college, with plans to get his associate degree and subsequently enter the military. I was proud of him for being honest with himself—and with me—about what he really wanted.

My second concern was that my job at the celebrity facial spa was becoming increasingly overwhelming. At first, I wasn't sure why. But I knew I couldn't keep everything straight—I felt like there was way too much information to juggle—which prompted me to dig deeper to find out why. So I made an appointment with an ADHD specialist.

The first few times I saw the specialist, she asked me a lot of questions. Naturally, she wanted to understand what had prompted me to reach out to her and what was going on in the present, specifically at work. But she also dug into my history, inquiring about such things as: Did I struggle academically when I was growing up? Did I get into trouble often in school? What did I get into trouble for?

As a result, she confirmed that I was suffering from a severe form of ADHD and prescribed medication to help.

It took months to get my dosage correct. I had to see her once every couple of weeks in the beginning, so she could observe my mannerisms and "telltale signs," as she called them. She said she could see my eyes darting around when we were speaking, and she noticed that I would get easily distracted or completely lose my train of thought in the middle of our conversations. Not to mention my constant fidgeting. Finally, after about six months, we settled on the right dosage for me. I was feeling less overwhelmed, but my issues weren't entirely fixed.

I worked hard to come up with new strategies to stay on point at my job, and in my life in general. I taught myself to write everything down so I wouldn't forget stuff. To this day, I set alarms to help me remember important pieces of information. If I'm going to be on my computer for work, there has to be a whole note system right in front of me. I can't keep it on my phone, because if my phone isn't open, then I won't see it and be reminded. The more things I have on my plate, and the more I'm being pulled in different directions, the more complicated things are for me. I have to constantly come up with new techniques to help me accomplish tasks so I don't drop the ball on anything. It's a big challenge, one that I still constantly struggle with and work hard to manage.

To make matters worse, my boss at the spa was exceptionally particular.

On the spur of the moment, she'd rush over to my desk and announce, "Kim Kardashian is on her way here. Stop whatever you're doing!"

"Oh, okay," I'd reply nervously, aware that a celebrity visit of this caliber would launch the entire office into a frenzy to accommodate whichever A-lister it was.

"Don't delay. We have a million things to do before she arrives," she'd urge, attempting to light a fire under me. It wasn't that I was lazy—far from it—I was just harried by having to pause one task and switch to another so abruptly.

Regardless of this hurdle, I loved everything about Manhattan—the frenetic energy, the fast pace, the restaurants, the culture, and so much more. I didn't get to go out that much while I lived there, because my budget was meager, but I did dine at some casual restaurants on the Upper East Side. I also enjoyed the Meatpacking District on the West Side because of the cobblestone streets and fun clubs. And there were some places along the Hudson River, where I'd get brunch or a drink and watch the boats. Being in New York not only was exhilarating but also provided a unique and welcome learning curve for me, as I believe most new experiences do. I wouldn't want to live for a long time again in New York, but at the time, it was the right home for me.

And even though things were tough financially, somehow Anna and I were able to make it work. By that point, she had another good job—at Skinney Medspa doing CoolSculpting—which she still does, only now in California. Anna is not only my sister but also my best friend, and I relished the freedom of being in an amazing city with her after such a horrible time in my life.

We made a few great friends, whom I'm still close with. One was a woman named Olivia who worked at the facial spa with me—I was the manager and she was the receptionist—while she was in medical school. I actually just saw her when I was in Manhattan for New York Fashion Week. Anna also had a boyfriend for much of the year and a half we lived there, and he introduced us to some of his friends.

Although I was still legally married to Drew, I considered myself single. While in New York, I dated two men, both doctors, whom I met on Tinder. They were very busy as residents back then, which was convenient for me, because I was doing my own thing and not looking to commit to anyone too seriously. I was all about working hard and having fun. And even though neither relationship worked out, I'm actually still friends with both of them.

Casual dating in New York—especially after my relationship with Drew—was an affirmative and empowering experience. I was starting to feel more confident, and enjoyed going out with Anna and just letting loose.

Looking back, there's one night that I'll never forget about my NYC experience, mainly because it was so spontaneous and random—and it felt like one of those "only in New York" moments. It was New Year's Eve 2014, I was thirty-four years old, and at the end of the night, after all the partying, Anna and I were walking down the street pretty intoxicated when we noticed a police car driving beside us.

Anna nudged me in the side with her elbow and whispered, "Shit, Mary, we're going to get in trouble for being drunk in public."

I was so nervous that when the car pulled over to the sidewalk, I smiled awkwardly, offered a little wave to the officers, and said, "Hi."

One of them smiled back and replied, "You beautiful ladies should not be out by yourselves this late at night; let us take you wherever you're going."

Anna and I looked at each other, let out sighs of relief, and accepted their offer. We actually ended up hanging out with them for a couple of hours and even snapping photos. It was, undoubtedly, one of our most unique experiences while living there.

But despite all the fun I was having, I was definitely a bit lost at this point in my life, and I had yet to find my way. I couldn't help but feel that everything had changed so drastically in such a short time. I'd gone from having this whole family life with Drew that was purportedly "normal," with a big house and a swimming pool. I'd been married, owned a business, and I was a mom, taking two kids to school each day and helping them with their homework at night. Then, suddenly, we'd moved to London, things had taken a horrible turn both emotionally and financially, and I was on my own again, with a husband who refused to divorce me and an empty bank account. It was a lot to digest and a steep hurdle to clear.

Honestly, I couldn't really pinpoint what I wanted, or where to go from there. I'd thought about real estate, because I'd done that in California, but it was a completely different industry in New York, where attorneys basically did everything and it was much harder to make money right away. I wasn't unhappy at the facial spa, but I wasn't truly happy there either. So, I decided to leave that job and do some waitressing and bartending until I figured out what to do next. It felt like I was always taking two steps forward, then three steps back, which got me nowhere.

By the end of July, right around the twenty-ninth—my birthday—I was feeling particularly down, and I really wanted to do something special. One of my dearest friends and old roommate Amanza was dating the actor Taye Diggs, and he bought me a round-trip ticket to LA so I could celebrate my birthday with her. I was beyond grateful for Taye's generosity and incredibly excited to escape from the status quo.

When I got there, Amanza asked her friend Jason Oppenheim (my current boss and the star of *Selling Sunset*) if he wanted to go to dinner with us. Jason and I had met once before—about a decade earlier, in 2004—at a barbecue at Amanza's house. I had been with Jeff at the time, but he had told Amanza that he thought I was really beautiful and jokingly referred to me as "Hot Mary." We hadn't been in touch since then.

When Amanza told Jason that "Hot Mary" was in town, he quickly accepted her dinner invitation. Of course, he had no idea I was still technically married—and to a different guy.

Before the dinner, Amanza and I got ready at Taye's place. Taye had recently split from his ex-wife, the actress Idina Menzel, and they were in the process of moving out of their house. Idina had left a bunch of stuff behind that she was planning to donate to charity, and I didn't have any nice shoes with me.

Amanza handed me the tallest pair of heels and said, "Idina is giving these away, try them on."

"I can't wear her shoes!" I protested, shocked by Amanza's offer. "I don't even know her."

Amanza made a face at me. "Don't be ridiculous, Mary. It will be fine."

"Are you sure?" I asked, still hesitant to "borrow" from this famous actress who had no clue that I was in her former home, even if she was planning on giving the shoes away anyway.

"I'm positive. You're going to look so hot in them. As I said, she's donating these anyway and they are brand-new."

I reluctantly agreed, and slid them onto my feet. Looking in the mirror, I smiled—Amanza was right, I did look hot in them. Then I took a step, and nearly fell. The heel was so high my ankles kept locking up when I tried to walk. After a few minutes of adjusting, I decided to keep them on—it was my birthday, after all, and they made me look really good.

We ended up all going out to dinner and then to a lounge-meets-nightclub spot afterward. As we were entering the club, I could feel myself teetering in Idina's stilettos.

Suddenly, I turned to Jason and said, "Oh God, oh God, I think I'm going to face-plant. I literally can't move!"

Jason immediately looped his arm through mine, helped me over to one of the couches, and sat me down. "Let's get these shoes off," he said. He helped me out of the heels and started to rub my feet and ankles.

"Thank you so much," I replied, grateful for his assistance and the extra attention. "That feels amazing."

"Better, babe?" He laughed easily. Jason definitely has a way with women, to say the least. And there was an instant connection between the two of us.

One thing led to another, and Jason and I ended up kissing that night. The next morning, as I was packing up to return to my life in New York, Jason called me at Amanza's house.

"I'm on your street. I'm coming to pick you up to take you to brunch," he said, as if we'd made a plan to get together.

"That's so sweet." I was truly flattered by the invitation and, more specifically, just happy to hear from him. "But I can't. I have a flight to catch."

"No worries, we're going to change your flight. You can leave later," he replied confidently.

"I'm so sorry, I really can't change it." I wanted to go out with him, but I knew it would be too expensive to switch my ticket, and I never would have asked Taye to pay for that too.

"I'm not exactly giving you a choice here. I want to spend time with you," he continued. "I'll take care of it." I found his assertiveness to be very attractive.

Of course, if I'd known then what I know now about Jason, I wouldn't have bothered to object! Once he sets his mind to something, it's happening, whether you like it or not. And, in this case, I liked it.

Over brunch, we ended up really clicking, and I stayed in LA an extra day. When I landed in New York, he called me and asked, "How soon can you come here again? I want to buy you a ticket."

For the next few weeks, I jetted back and forth between New York and LA. If you can believe it, Jason kept paying my colleagues at the restaurant where I worked, in the Financial District, to cover my shifts so I could visit him more often.

Jason was working really hard launching The Oppenheim Group out of his house. He was a one-man show, which meant it was much easier for me to go to LA than for him to come to NYC. But, finally, the travel became overwhelming and impossible for me, so we decided I'd move to LA, with my sidekick Niko in tow, to live with Jason and find a new job out there. Though our courtship had been less than a month long, I was in love. More to the point, I knew straightaway that Jason was meant to be in my life one way or another.

When I told Anna, I remember her saying to me, "What is wrong with you? Have you learned nothing from past experiences? You can't just upend your life and move across the country for some random guy."

I replied, "I can't explain it. It just makes sense."

To be clear, I completely understood her perspective—who wouldn't? But my gut instinct was telling me it was right.

I knew I couldn't be apart from Jason. I'd fallen head over heels for him. The thing about Jason is that, when he's all in, he makes you feel like you're the most important person on the face of the earth, the only person who exists in his world, and it's totally authentic. He's an amazing boyfriend and a genuinely compassionate and caring person. When he loves somebody, he will love them forever.

There were definitely plenty of people who were skeptical and surprised that Jason was living with a woman, but I didn't see it, nor did I care.

Nevertheless, things were great with us for four solid months. In my mind, everything was smooth sailing. What I didn't realize was that Jason had started to feel pressured to settle down with me. But he never mentioned it or even displayed signs that he was concerned.

It wasn't until many years later that Jason confided his real feelings throughout that time.

"I was trying to pick fights with you so that we'd break up organically or so you'd want to break up with me," he said. "But you wouldn't take the bait!"

When he shared this with me, I thought it was so amusing, because I had no recollection of him doing that. "I assumed you were just in a bad mood every now and then, and I'd let you blow off steam. I didn't allow it to affect me at all and was totally unaware that it was a tactic."

In retrospect, the signs from Jason were pretty obvious, but I probably didn't notice what was going on because I was distracted by finally pursuing a divorce from Drew. Despite Jason's attempts to split us up, he was giving me really helpful advice on how to separate from Drew without his consent.

One afternoon, right around this stage, Jason and I went to get our nails done, which was something we did often. I was talking to him about the whole Drew predicament and saying how I didn't even know where Drew was or how to contact him. Jason had a few suggestions about specific ways to go after Drew, but I didn't want to take his advice. "Drew is a loose cannon," I explained. "I don't want to dredge up any old drama."

"Okay, I understand that, but you want the divorce, right?" Jason asked, pragmatically.

"I do, but I don't trust him at all," I replied. He'd never met Drew, so he had no idea what a manipulator he could be.

"I get it." He nodded. "I still think you should try what I recommended."

"I don't know." I shook my head. "I don't want you to get involved. I'd feel terrible if it backfired and jeopardized you or your business."

Well, that was all it took to set Jason off. Seemingly out of nowhere, he lost his shit.

He screamed, "What the hell, Mary? I can't believe you'd put me or my company at risk like this."

"I didn't say you were at risk." I tried to keep my voice down and hoped he would too, since we were in a public place. "I just said, I'd never *want* to put you at risk."

"This is crazy! I can't believe you'd do this to me." Without warning, he shot to his feet and made a beeline toward the front door of the salon.

"Jason, wait!" I called after him.

He turned toward me and yelled, "I want you out of my house! You have two hours."

And then he stormed out, leaving me sitting there in the nail salon, alone and in total shock. I burst into tears. I had no idea what had happened to incite his over-the-top reaction.

Honestly, that was the biggest fight Jason and I have ever had, though I was never scared. Even when Jason gets upset, he's the most loving, caring person you could ever meet.

Many years later, he reflected on his true feelings in that moment and explained the outburst. "After trying to pick fights with you for weeks, to no avail, I seized the opportunity you'd placed in my lap to blow things up. I'm so sorry. I really am. I simply couldn't bring myself to tell you that I didn't want to commit anymore."

He further clarified, "When I believe that someone or something might threaten everything I've worked so hard for, I go ballistic. I never thought that you intended to hurt me, nor did I want to hurt you; I was merely using the circumstance as a chance to extract myself from being tied down."

Jason is very self-aware when it comes to his own limitations and what he's capable of. Still, at the time, I didn't understand what his motives were, and I was hysterical. I drove directly to Amanza's, crying like a baby the whole way. I remember pulling into her driveway and her running out to the car, like a scene from a movie. She hugged me and comforted me as I wept in her arms. It was super dramatic.

"He's a fucking asshole," she declared, even though Jason was originally her friend.

"I don't even know what happened," I bawled. "One minute we were getting manicures and the next minute he was freaking out at me."

"He screamed at you in front of other people?" Amanza huffed. She was instantly defensive on my behalf.

"Yes." I sniffed.

"That's it. He's done. I'm not speaking to him." She walked me inside. "I can't believe he'd treat you this way."

"I can't either. He's never done anything like this." I swallowed a sob.

"Let me tell you something," Amanza continued. "No one messes with my best friend and gets away with it."

The funny thing is that even once I'd forgiven Jason, which was pretty quickly, Amanza continued to boycott him. She felt responsible for introducing the two of us and was pissed that he'd betrayed her trust in him, so she refused to talk to him for a full year. That's the kind of friend she is—the one you want in your corner.

I lived with Amanza for a few months after Jason kicked me out, even though he and I dated on and off for another six months—which added up to a year in total—but it was never entirely exclusive again. Unfortunately, I didn't fully realize that until one particular night when we were out at a bar, and I saw him kissing a woman, directly in my line of sight, which was really screwed up. I loved Jason, and if he no longer wanted to be with just me, I wanted to know that. It felt like our relationship was simply too much, too soon, for him, even though we'd been together for a while.

Once they'd finished making out, I marched up to him and said, "What is wrong with you? Why are you inviting me on your dates?" Regardless of my rocky history with men, I'd never allow a man to disrespect me in that way, even though I now know Jason's intentions weren't bad.

"It's not a date," he answered, nonchalantly. "We're all hanging out. It's no big deal."

"Well, it's a big deal to me," I said. "I can't do this anymore. It's messing with my mind."

When I left the bar that night, I knew I had to put space between us, if Jason and I were going to be able to remain friends in the future, which I wanted, since we were great friends, despite our romantic history. Our lives were just too entwined because we were in the same social circle and shared custody of our dogs, Niko and Zelda.

At the time, I was working as an assistant to Amanza's boyfriend, Taye. It was a temporary gig until I could pursue real estate fully, and it was also a tricky situation, since Taye was dating one of my closest friends. For example, when they were fighting and Amanza would want to know where he was, I couldn't tell her because I had confidentiality obligations to Taye.

The good news for all of us was that, in July 2015, Taye ended up landing the title role in *Hedwig and the Angry Inch* on

Broadway, so I went with him to New York for a few months. It was exactly the opportunity I needed to get over Jason, although he did visit me while I was there. We couldn't stay away from each other! Even though we never hooked up romantically again, this led us to figure out that we were better as friends, and we've been the closest friends ever since.

Ultimately, once Taye's Broadway run was over, I returned to California. At about the same time, Jason bought a triplex in LA that he planned to rent as furnished units, but he didn't want to deal with the details himself. He asked if I'd be willing to handle all of the renovations and the decorating in exchange for living in one of them at a reduced rent. It was a generous offer and a great deal, especially since I had nowhere else to go, so I said yes.

On the work front, I dove headfirst into real estate. I was studying to renew my license, which I'd let lapse for too long, so Jason hired me to work part-time at The Oppenheim Group. I helped out in the office, sent mailers, and did other basic tasks. I was also assisting a very successful female agent at Compass and bartending at night in West Hollywood, at a restaurant called Katana.

Basically, I was back to working three jobs, trying to keep my head above water, and still single as ever.

I felt like I was starting from scratch. Yet again.

6

Rock Bottom

It was Memorial Day weekend and I was completely alone, with no significant other and no plans. Amanza was with Taye in New York, and all of my other friends were in Malibu, where Jason was throwing a big holiday bash. Under normal circumstances, I would have been there with them, but Jason didn't want me to come due to the fact that he was bringing a date. He preferred to be able to hook up with other women guilt-free and without throwing it in my face. While I appreciated the intention behind his decision, I felt left out and forsaken.

I wasn't dating anyone at the time, mainly because I was busy juggling three jobs, from 7:00 a.m. until 2:00 a.m. the following day, and I also hadn't met anyone who'd piqued my interest.

Money was still tight, and I was working my butt off to pay my bills and save so I could get back on track. Between the three jobs, and what felt like constant changes in my life, I was struggling to get ahead. I had big goals—primarily to be financially stable enough to quit two of my three jobs and focus my energy entirely on real estate. But it felt like nothing was ever pushing forward.

Since my friends were out of town, I decided that getting a tattoo would be a welcome distraction—my eighth, if you can believe it! While I was getting my tattoo, my phone buzzed. It was a text from Joe—an acquaintance of Amanza who was looking to see what my plans were for the weekend. He was a bartender and on the shorter side. Joe told me that he and his friend Luke—who was a pretty cute guy whom Amanza and I had hung out with a couple of times—were going to meet at his apartment and then go out with a fun group. I didn't know Joe or Luke that well, but I figured, why not? I thought Luke was cool, and I had nothing better to do. So, after my tattoo was finished, I went over to Joe's place to hang out until Luke arrived.

"Hey, come on in." Joe opened the door to his apartment, a modest bachelor pad in downtown LA.

"Thanks." I stepped inside and surveyed my surroundings. There was a small kitchen and a single bedroom off the main room. A few simple pieces of furniture were scattered about. It was enough space for one person to live comfortably.

"Take a seat." He motioned to the couch.

"Is Luke on his way?" I asked Joe as I lowered myself onto one of the leather cushions.

"Yeah, he should be here pretty soon." Joe walked into the kitchen. "How about a drink in the meantime?"

"Okay, sure." I smiled.

A minute later he returned with a little French wineglass filled with a bright blue liquid and handed it to me. "Here you go. It's a vodka cocktail."

"Thanks." I took the glass from him as he joined me on the sofa. Aside from the vodka, I had no idea what I was drinking, but it was such a small amount of booze that I knew I wouldn't get drunk.

Joe and I chatted about nothing in particular for about twenty minutes, but I started to wonder what was delaying Luke. I wasn't concerned. Joe seemed like a nice enough guy, and I was just ready to get on with the night.

"Is Luke definitely coming?" I asked, directly.

"I think so." Joe didn't make eye contact.

"You're not sure?" I cocked my head. "I thought you said he was on the way."

"Yeah, yeah," Joe answered vaguely. He quickly changed the subject by asking, "Do you want to go outside and smoke a cigarette?"

"I guess." I was kind of confused, because Joe wasn't a smoker himself, but I chalked it up to politeness.

"You don't have to go all the way downstairs. There's a window at the end of the hallway. You can crack it open."

"Great." I exited his apartment and did as he suggested. When I returned he was still sitting on the couch where I'd left him, and we made small talk for a while longer as I drained my vodka cocktail.

Joe then told me Luke wasn't actually going to join us and continued to recount a very bizarre story, which should have been my first warning sign that things were not right.

"So, there was this girl I had sex with," he said, as if I were some fraternity brother he was bragging to. "She was really hot.

I just threw her down, even though she didn't really want it. But I didn't care."

"What are you talking about?" I looked at him like he was crazy, even though he didn't seem to notice.

"Yeah, well, I wanted to fuck her."

"Do you know how fucked-up that is?" I asked, alarmed by his blasé attitude. "Don't ever say that to anybody else."

Suddenly I realized that my mind was getting fuzzy, and my eyelids were growing heavy.

"It wasn't a big deal." He shrugged.

"That's a huge deal," I countered. I couldn't process what I was hearing. It sounded an awful lot like he was admitting he'd taken advantage of this woman. Yet, strangely, I still didn't view him as a predator. As I became woozier and woozier I just thought perhaps I'd misunderstood him.

"Whatever." He smirked.

"Can I please have some water?" My mouth was unusually parched.

"You sure you don't want another drink instead?" He stood up.

"No, I just need water."

He headed into the kitchen, and when he came back— seemingly out of nowhere—I started to cry.

"What the hell is wrong with you?" He regarded me with distaste.

"I want to be with Jason and my friends," I replied, thinking about how brokenhearted I was that they were all off having a blast without me.

That's the last thing I remember saying before I passed out.

When I woke up, I was on Joe's bed, with my arms pinned against his mattress, and my pants around my ankles.

He was on top of me and inside of me.

"Get the fuck off!" I shouted, kicking and screaming as I desperately tried to figure out what was going on. I couldn't see straight. I couldn't think straight. Everything was a blur.

"Stop, you want it." He kept repeating that one sentence, until—finally—by some miracle I was able to free myself from his grip.

I ran out of his apartment as fast as I could. Thank God he didn't chase after me. I went straight to my car and sat there bawling and shaking for what felt like forever but was probably only a few minutes. Then I realized, despite my fogginess, that I needed to get out of there fast. I didn't want to stay in that location for fear that he'd come looking for me, so I drove a couple of streets away and pulled over to the side of the road. I was hyperventilating, and the world appeared to be spinning around me. Honestly, I'm not sure how long I sat there. All I know is that, eventually, I was able to drive myself home.

In hindsight, I should have gone directly to the hospital, but I was ashamed and scared and in complete shock. As soon as I got back to my house, I took the longest, hottest shower of my life. I scrubbed my skin so hard that I thought it might tear off.

I didn't say a word to anyone. I went into total survival mode, even though I was a wreck on the inside. Joe had violated me in the worst possible way, and I was horrified that someone would find out.

It wasn't until Amanza returned from New York with Taye after the holiday weekend and called to check in that I had to confront my demon.

"What are you doing tomorrow night?" she asked. "Let's go out and have fun."

"I don't know," I said apathetically. I'd been wearing the same pair of pajamas for days and had barely gotten out of bed. I couldn't even remember if I'd eaten anything.

"What's wrong?" As soon as Amanza heard my voice, she could tell something was off.

"Nothing." I didn't want to think about what had happened, much less talk about it. I told myself it was my fault for even going to Joe's apartment alone. Why had I allowed myself to do that? Why had I thought it was okay? I barely knew him, and I should have been more responsible.

"Is this about Jason?"

"No, no; it's fine, really. I'm okay." I tried to sound convincing.

"Let's go out then. It'll lift your spirits," Amanza nudged.

"Sure, I guess." It was the last thing I wanted to do, but I also didn't want to tip her off that something was wrong.

So, the following evening Amanza, Taye, and I ended up at a bar in West Hollywood. As I stood there, drink in hand, wondering how soon I could leave, I spotted him from across the bar.

Joe. My rapist.

I must have turned paler than a ghost, because Amanza took one look at me and said, "Mary, what's happening? Do you feel okay?" She followed my stare until her eyes locked on him.

"Um, I, uh . . ." I couldn't speak. My body just started to quiver and sway.

She could tell right away from my body language and how visibly shaken up I was that something was really wrong.

"Motherfucker. What did he do to you?" She knew immediately. "Please, Mary, tell me this isn't what I think it is! Look at me. I need you to tell me what's going on. Did he do what I think?" Amanza knew this panicked look all too well, and she knew me well enough to read the trauma I was trying my best to conceal.

I nodded my head without saying a word.

"Let's go right now. We're getting you out of here." Amanza grabbed my hand and then called Taye over. She explained what was going on and said that we'd be outside waiting for him.

I later found out that Taye had spoken to management at the bar and told them in no uncertain terms that Joe was a threat to women and never to allow him back into the bar again.

I loved that Amanza and Taye wanted to protect me. But no amount of shelter could cure me. I was damaged goods. And terrified that I'd never be able to be happy again.

For years, there were instances when I'd see someone who looked like Joe and have a full-blown panic attack. I'll never forget one specific instance, shortly after the rape, when I was driving to the office, getting ready to turn onto Sunset Boulevard, and there was this guy walking out of a parking lot. At first glance, his silhouette resembled Joe's. I couldn't breathe. I pulled over to the side of the road and called Jason. I can't explain why, other than that I needed a trusted friend and to feel safe.

"Oh my God, Mary, what is it? Are you okay?" he asked as soon as he heard the panic in my voice.

"No!" I cried.

"Where are you? Can you make it to my house?"

"I think so," I told him, and I did.

As soon as I got there, I shared with Jason what had happened, and he was so supportive and comforting.

After that, Amanza and Taye took me with them when they left a few days later for New York, so I could get away. I kept trying to act like things were okay, but they knew I needed to leave town. I needed someplace that felt safe.

Again, while the respite was welcome, it didn't fix me. Nothing could fix me.

The repercussions of that night still haunt me. I never go to people's houses that I don't know. I won't be alone with any man that I haven't been friends with for at least five years or who's 100 percent gay, so I know I'm safe. I won't go to parties if there are going to be a bunch of random people there, even if I'm at Jason's house. I'm in therapy for it with the hope that, one day, I'll be healed.

Often, I remind myself of the tattoo that was etched on my forearm on that fateful day.

It says BUT THE FIGHTER STILL REMAINS. How's that for irony?

7

Turning Point

What do I do when I hit rock bottom? I dust myself off and reassemble the pieces of my life. For as long as I can remember my mantra has been: If you don't like your current situation, then change it. I've never been afraid to take a chance or switch things up when I'm unhappy, and I truly believe there's a solution to almost every problem. For me, in order to keep moving, I try to stay positive and make sure my focus is on the right place, even if it means I have to work harder, give up certain benefits (like financial security), and take a leap of faith.

This was my exact mindset when I transitioned from part-time to full-time at The Oppenheim Group in 2016. I knew my other two jobs as a personal assistant and bartender were starting to get in the way of my real estate career. One day, after I was forced to turn down a client because I was committed to a shift at Katana, I realized something had to change. I needed to concentrate all of my efforts on real estate if I wanted the opportunity to pursue my passion and bring in serious money. I figured I could always go back and find another assistant or bartending gig if I had to, although I hoped I wouldn't need to.

Jason also played a major role in this decision—he went out of his way to ensure I was making enough money at The Oppenheim Group and encouraged me to quit my other jobs.

"Mary, you have to take a chance," he said. "I'll help you in any way I can."

I knew he was right, but I was also aware of the risks. "I just need to be sure I can support myself," I replied. "As you well know, selling multimillion-dollar homes doesn't happen overnight."

But Jason—in typical fashion—was persistent. "Here's what I can do," he continued. "I'll pay you to host open houses and showings for me, so you'll have a little bit of extra income. I can pay you to handle some assistant work for me too."

I was so grateful for his generosity, though I didn't want special treatment. "That would be amazing," I replied. "But only if it makes sense for the brokerage."

"I'd be paying someone else anyway," he pointed out. "You can consider it done."

At this point in my life, I knew I had to sink or swim. And I was ready to swim across the English Channel if I had to. So, I said, "Okay, I'm in!"

I committed myself 100 percent and never looked back. As I started establishing myself, Jason continued to be a very supportive boss, motivating me to dive in and take on more and more. I held open houses for him every Sunday. Then on the following Tuesdays, I would research all of the new homes that had hit the market. This way, if there were clients who didn't love any of the open houses, I had alternate properties ready to show them. That was how I started to build my Rolodex.

I was in the office every single day—one of the first agents to arrive and one of the last to leave. I'd wake up in the morning and immediately go on the Multiple Listing Service (MLS). I wanted to have a running catalog in my head of everything that was for sale, everything that had recently sold, and the corresponding price points, so that I was completely informed about the area. This also allowed me to find properties for current clients who were looking to buy and to understand the best way to showcase homes that were for sale. I'd then head out to all of the brokers' open houses so I could create videos for social media and get my name out there, or I'd tag along with Jason to his showings. If anyone asked me if I'd seen a specific house, not only could I say yes, but I'd also be armed with all of the information necessary to make a deal.

When I was first starting out, I knew I had to be a sponge and absorb the maximum amount of information I could from my experienced colleagues. I watched and listened to how they operated because I knew they were doing something right. Also, as a newer agent in a new area, I was very careful not to develop an ego. My feeling is: there's always more to learn and, in order to acquire the wisdom necessary to succeed on my own, I wanted to keep pushing myself.

It took at least a month to find my first client, and when I did, the listing was an eight-million-dollar home in Bel Air, which was a huge coup for me. The seller's previous agent had been his mother, and she wasn't moving the property, so I came in and recommended some changes, the most significant being to drop the price from nine million to eight million, which was what it was actually worth. I also convinced him to stage the property and paint a few items to modernize it more. Fortunately, my recommendations must have been good, because the seller then received multiple offers, which were all close to the new asking price. But, ultimately, it wasn't enough money for him and he got cold feet, so he decided to pull the home off the market.

It was an extremely frustrating experience for me—it was my first client since starting at The Oppenheim Group and I was so excited to land what I thought was going to be a major deal. I also liked the seller very much as a person, but as a client he was complicated, because he changed his mind all the time. I did my job, I got the offers, and then he reneged, which was very frustrating. I couldn't understand why he wasn't up-front with me from the onset. If he knew that a near asking price offer wasn't going to satisfy him, why bother making me spin my wheels?

I'd also invested a lot of money on marketing—we typically split that expense with Jason—which seemed like a waste. Fortunately, Jason was kind enough to cover all of it.

"It's not your fault," he said. "You did everything right, so I'll absorb the marketing costs." Jason knew I didn't have the money. Not every boss would understand that.

I told myself that losing the deal wasn't personal, and that clients have the right to change their minds, but it still stung. The thing about real estate is that for every transaction that goes south, there's another one that falls into your lap. Sometimes deals come so easily that it's almost silly how much money you can make with very little effort. In other cases, you can bend over backward for a client for two years and then they'll want to rethink things or, even worse, hire another agent. It's hard not to be injured by that, but I learned quickly to develop a thick skin.

I know that I'm always doing the best that I can and always trying my hardest, often going above and beyond for my clients. But I can't control other people, which is why, when a deal does come through, I'm always smart about saving my money, because I never know when the next deal is going to happen. This way, when I do experience a setback, I'll have a little nest egg to rely on.

Thankfully, after the eight-million-dollar deal fell through, I went on to sell a three-million-dollar house in West Hollywood. Things really started to take off from there. Since I no longer had Austin living with me (he was already nineteen years old and fully ensconced in college), I was able to devote all of my time to my career, and I was determined to prove myself. I was sick of changing jobs and uprooting my life, and I knew that if I continued to hustle—even though it was going to require long hours and endless patience—I could make something of myself.

One of the most effective means of expanding your knowledge and expertise is to find a mentor who's willing to guide you as you pursue your goals. For me, that person has always been Jason. Along the way, I relied heavily on Jason's advice and guidance. I saw how successful he was, and I wanted that for myself. Not only is he my boss and former boyfriend, but he's also one of my closest friends. And he acts as a trusted adviser and confidant in all areas of my life. What many people don't realize is that Jason is a contractor and an attorney, in addition to being a real estate icon. Basically, he's brilliant.

I learn more and more from him every day, which has been an invaluable asset in growing my career. I feel truly lucky to have someone like Jason to bounce ideas off, and I can ask him as many questions as I need. I'm consistently in awe of how he thinks outside the box and comes up with creative solutions that I wouldn't necessarily have thought of. If ever I get stuck with some aspect of a deal, he's the first person I call.

With that said, our methods are not always the same. For example, Jason is far more direct than I'm comfortable with. He relies on brutal honesty at all times.

I remember one instance when we walked into a client's home and he said (to the client!) something like, "This furniture is absolutely awful; you have to get rid of it and stage the house if you want it to sell."

I pulled him aside and said, "Jason—those are this man's personal items. He *chose* them. You can't offend him like that."

And Jason replied, "Trust me, I know what I'm talking about. He'll thank me later."

So I went back to the client and reframed Jason's words. I explained, "What Jason meant is that the furniture has a very specific style and we need it to appeal to the widest range of buyers."

Jason laughed, shook his head, and said, "Nope, I actually meant it looks like shit."

I'll admit there have been times when being nice hasn't been entirely effective for me, and I've relied on Jason to insert himself and be a bit more forceful. That's one of the reasons I look up to him, even though I also rely on my own instincts.

His advice to me has always been: "Be yourself. People trust authenticity. And really listen to what your clients want. Then read between those lines. As an agent, you have to be an observer. It's your job to notice when their eyes light up or when they grimace at something."

In addition to Jason's support, I also had—and still have—great camaraderie with my colleagues. When I first started working at The Oppenheim Group, there were already several agents on staff. There was Jason's twin brother, Brett Oppenheim, along with Maya Vander, Heather Rae Young (now Heather Rae El Moussa), and Nicole Young. Though many people may have found it intimidating or nerve-racking to join such a powerful group of men and women, I fit in from the very beginning, in part because I didn't come in guns blazing or view them as direct competition.

I already knew Nicole, since we'd met through mutual friends and she'd dated Jason before I did, but I had no previous relationships with the other ladies. I'm a girl's girl through and through. I believe in supporting my colleagues and celebrating their wins—that's the culture I try to maintain at The Oppenheim Group, and it's reflective of the way I live my life.

From day one, I loved and respected my colleagues, and felt accepted by them in return. We still hang out together during business and social hours, we travel in a group, often with our partners, and we're truly happy when any one of us lands a big deal or realizes success either personally or professionally.

In my experience, it's so much better to rally around the people you work with rather than to view them as your rivals. Instead of envying their accomplishments, I use their triumphs to motivate me. If I see my colleagues doing really well and selling a lot of homes, it inspires me to step up my own game. If you project negativity, that's what you'll receive in return, which will not help you grow your career. During my time at The Oppenheim Group, there have been only a few agents who didn't understand our cooperative style and who acted jealous whenever anyone else flourished. They're no longer with us for that reason.

One of those agents was Christine Quinn. Christine came on board a few months after I did—her boyfriend was working with us at the time and facilitated the opportunity, since it was her first foray into real estate.

At first, Christine seemed totally normal, and we became fast friends. She would hang out with me and Nicole quite often, and we even attended Nicole's wedding together. There were some red flags—I did think it was a little strange and over-the-top when she told me she only wanted to date men who were multimillionaires—but I also thought she was fun, and she made me laugh. There was never a dull moment with Christine, for better or for worse—although the worse hadn't reared its ugly head . . . yet.

*O*verall, 2016 was a very happy time for me. Work was going well. I had plenty of friends. And I finally felt that in my near future I would be financially secure. The singular piece missing from the puzzle was a significant other, until I met Roger on Bumble. He was an accountant and appeared great on paper—smart, clean-cut, and handsome with gorgeous green eyes. He was also kind of nerdy, in a good way, which made me think he was a nice, safe guy.

He was my first serious boyfriend since dating Jason, and we got serious pretty quickly. After three months, we were living together. Then months later I found out he had cheated on me.

I could sense things weren't right. In part, it was a gut instinct, but it was also little details of stories he'd tell me that didn't add up, so I approached him and said, "I feel like there's something you're hiding from me."

Immediately, he replied, "I don't know what you're talking about."

And I was like, "Come on. I'm not stupid. I'd rather you just be honest with me so we can work through whatever it is. I don't like secrets."

At that, he grew silent. I watched his face get red and prepared myself for what he was about to confess.

"I cheated on you," he blurted, with a sigh of guilt-meets-relief.

I took a long, deep breath and tried not to flip out. "Okay. What happened?"

"I was at this event. You weren't around. I was drinking. One thing led to another. And I invited this woman back to our house."

"You cheated on me in our house?!" I shrieked. So much for not flipping out.

"Yes," he acknowledged, sheepishly.

"Please tell me you didn't sleep with her in our bed."

He didn't answer. He didn't have to.

"When was this?" I questioned, intent on gleaning all the details, even though I knew every word out of his lying mouth would make me angrier. I didn't care.

"Right before we went to Costa Rica," he said, adding insult to injury.

"You mean when I took you there for your birthday? Are you out of your mind?!"

"I'm so sorry, Mary. It was a huge mistake. Please forgive me. It'll never happen again. I swear. I love you."

I refused to accept his apology. At first. But, like an idiot, I ultimately forgave him, only to be burned again.

Roger had been engaged to a woman four years before I came into the picture. She'd disappeared from his life without explanation, leaving their relationship somewhat open-ended. But while we were dating, she reached out to him, and I encouraged him to return her call. I honestly didn't believe he still had feelings for her, and for his benefit—and ours as a couple—I wanted him to understand what had happened and seek closure. Big mistake.

Once they'd reconnected, he started acting really odd. He'd go out for the night and not come home, and I was fed up with his irresponsible, disrespectful behavior.

The pattern continued, and one day, after he'd been out all night, I decided enough was enough. It was time to end things. I packed up all of my stuff, dramatically ripped the curtains I had picked out and paid for off the wall, and grabbed a bunch of other items I didn't want him to have. It was his place, but I'd paid to redecorate it, and I was feeling particularly petty, for good reason! I waited until he finally came home the next morning and confronted him.

"Where the hell have you been?" I asked, my hands planted firmly on my hips.

"Out," he replied, nonchalantly. He had no excuse, nor did he feel the need to supply one.

"Out? That's it?" I laughed bitterly. "Well, you know what? You can keep your bachelor lifestyle. I'm done."

Later that year, I found out that Roger married his former fiancée and that she was pregnant with their baby.

Once again, I needed somewhere new to live, which really hurt, because I'd already moved and been cheated on more times than I could count on both hands.

Christine knew what I was going through and asked if I wanted to stay at her place for a couple of weeks while I figured things out.

I thought that was an extremely compassionate gesture, and since I didn't have many options, I accepted her offer.

I ended up living with Christine for much longer than a couple of weeks, mainly because we got along really well and enjoyed each other's company. I was struggling to get over my breakup with Roger, and Christine was a solid friend to me. I'll never forget that.

Still, even with Christine's support, I was feeling so down and alone. Not surprisingly, Jason came to the rescue yet again.

At the time, he was in Paris with his brother, Brett. They were attending the wedding of one of our colleagues, Marie Charlotte, who happened to be French. He called me to check in on how I was doing after the split with Roger.

"I don't know. I guess I'm okay. Whatever," I told him. I didn't want to give Roger any more attention than he warranted.

Of course, Jason could tell by the sound of my voice that I was anything but okay. So he said, "You know what? Pack your bags. I'm flying you out here. Brett and I are heading directly to the south of France after the wedding to have some fun. You're coming with us. You're going to get your mind off this guy. He's a piece of shit."

"I don't know . . ." I responded. I didn't think I was capable of having fun. My mind wasn't in that place.

"Mary, just grab your passport, throw a few things in a suitcase, and hop in an Uber. I just booked your flight and it's leaving in a few hours. Don't miss it!" Jason insisted, as per usual.

And I knew he was right. So, I flew overseas to spend a few days with Jason and Brett and to distract myself from Roger.

Little did I know that, while I was in France, I would get a text that would change my life. It was from a potential client I'd been introduced to by a mutual friend. He was moving to town from Paris himself, and I was supposed to show him apartments in Los Angeles. I didn't know a thing about him. I hadn't even seen a photo. All I knew was that his name was Romain Bonnet.

Let's just say, things got significantly better from there. Roger who?

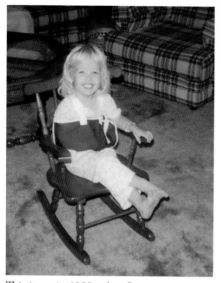

This is me in 1982, when I was two years old. It's one of the many times during my childhood when my arm was pulled out of its socket because I was so rambunctious. The ER doctors finally taught my dad how to pop it back in the socket to save us from frequent hospital trips!

I love this snapshot of my sisters and me with our dad, in 1986, on the beach in St. Augustine, Florida. We were visiting my great-aunt.

My family of five at my great-aunt's house in 1986, on summer vacation in Florida. We also went to SeaWorld and spent many days frolicking on the beach.

I was six years old here, and it was my first time seeing the ocean, in Jacksonville Beach, Florida.

Here I am in 1985, at five years old, with my sisters—Sarah, seven, and Anna, three— outside of our childhood home in Anderson, Indiana. It was my first day of kindergarten at St. Ambrose Catholic School.

At age seven, I took my First Communion at St. Ambrose Catholic Church.

My initial attempt at entrepreneurship, in June 1988, with my younger sister, Anna, at our childhood home in Anderson. My family was hosting a summer garage sale, and Anna and I decided to try our hand at a lemonade stand.

My dad and Granny
Babbitt in 1993 at my
aunt's house.

My cheerleading photo from
South Side Middle School in
Muncie, Indiana. I was thirteen
years old here.

I was a baby with a baby, eight months'
pregnant with my son, Austin, at only
sixteen years old. I didn't know I was
going to have a boy yet!

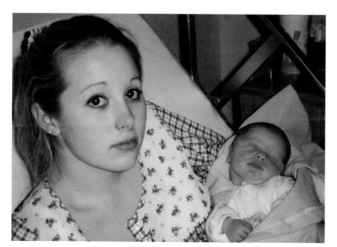

This is at the hospital
in Noblesville, Indiana,
in March 1997, after I
gave birth to Austin.
At sixteen, I was
still a child, who was
suddenly responsible
for another child. It's
crazy to look back and
realize just how young
and unprepared I was
for such an enormous
responsibility—though
I wouldn't change my
decision to become a
mom.

My mom spending time with her grandbabies—my son, Austin, and his first cousin, Rebecca (my sister Sarah's daughter)—in 1997, at our house in Lapel, Indiana.

Me with Austin on his first Christmas, in 1997, at my family's home in Lapel. He was nine months old and had just learned to stand. He loved opening all of his presents!

In 2000, with singer Brad Fischetti from the pop and hip hop band LFO. We casually dated for a while, and he'd invited me to one of their concerts in Indiana. Small world, Nick Cannon (Bre's baby daddy) was the MC at the event.

Me and best friend Shelly, at eighteen, singing karaoke in her mom's boyfriend's basement. Apparently, I've always been a fan of karaoke!

Anna's first trip to LA to visit me, after I'd moved there in 2002, when I was twenty-two years old. In order to save money on rent, Austin, Amanza, and I were living with Amanza's friend Andy (whom I eventually dated).

Anna and me, in 2004, at a sex shop called Pleasure Chest in West Hollywood, CA. I'm not sure what the specific occasion was, but we were definitely having a good time!

Me with Austin and my amazing stepsons-to-be, before Jeff and I were married. We were visiting the Mission San Juan Capistrano, a historic landmark and museum in Orange County.

Christmas 2005, with Austin, at my mom's house in Noblesville, Indiana. He was eight years old at the time.

Just after we moved to London, in December 2011, I took Austin on a sightseeing tour and then to France to show him many of the iconic and historical spots in Western Europe.

With my late first husband in 2004 at Jonathan Club in Santa Monica. We went with his law partner and his wife for a luau.

A few weeks after moving back to Scottsdale, Arizona, from London, in 2013, and visiting Austin for the holidays. He'd been living with my mom to finish high school while I extracted myself from my marriage to Drew.

With my sisters in Indiana, in July 2013, after my older sister's husband had, very sadly, passed away. We were trying to distract the kids and lift everyone's spirits by attending the local summer fair. After we left, I grabbed a bottle of terrible vodka, and we sat on my sister's kitchen floor, drank, and told funny stories to honor my late brother-in-law, Steve.

I'll never forget this night! It was New Year's Eve of 2014 in New York City, where I was living with Anna at the time. We were with the kind NYPD officers who graciously offered to take us home, because we were pretty drunk and freezing on the sidewalk. I had to get a photo so we could look back at it and laugh!

This was Halloween 2014, when Amanza and I dressed up as husband and wife and took our kids trick or treating. The funny thing is that we act like a married couple in real life!

Flanked by Brett and Jason in South America for New Year's 2015. We went to Argentina for a few days, then spent a week in Punta del Este, Uruguay. This was a few months after I'd moved out of Jason's house, but we were still "hooking up" in a more casual way.

Me in New York City in July 2015, while working for Amanza's boyfriend, Taye Diggs, during his run in *Hedwig and the Angry Inch* on Broadway. I'd moved back to Manhattan temporarily to help him while he played that demanding role. It was a very cool experience to be a part of.

Spending time with Amanza, who would fly to New York to visit Taye every few weeks while he was starring in *Hedwig and the Angry Inch*. Jason was also there on this occasion, so we all hung out and watched Taye perform. We took this photo backstage in Taye's dressing room.

This is Doheny, one of my favorite listings to date, second only to my wedding venue. It's a $28.5M home that has graced the cover of *Architectural Digest* and is truly a one-of-a-kind masterpiece that defines sophistication, tasteful design, and luxury living at its finest. *(Photo credit: Noel Kleinman)*

The Oppenheim Group team lunch back in 2016, before *Selling Sunset* started. Since the beginning, we've enjoyed going out to meals together.

Jason in rare form, in October 2019, after returning from Romain's bachelor party in Las Vegas. I guess they had fun!

Me and Austin spending Christmas together a few years ago with Romain, Jason, and Chrishell (not shown). Chrishell's dog Gracie, however, was not camera shy, joining our dogs Niko and Zelda.

In August 2015, I moved Austin into his dorm at University of Arizona, where he initially studied biochemistry. I remember feeling young to have a child in college, but I was so proud of him.

Romain at my thirty-seventh birthday party, in July 2017, at one of Jason's homes. We'd just begun dating two weeks earlier. This was the first time he got to know all of my friends, aside from Jason and Brett, whom he'd met on our first official date at Catch LA.

Romain and I secretly tied the knot on March 9, 2018, at the Ventura County Courthouse, but didn't tell anyone other than our closest friends. We wanted to have a real wedding that family could attend when the time was right and we were able to plan everything properly. We celebrated by getting amazing donuts afterward. Typical us, happy with the simple things in life.

Our wedding day! October 12, 2019. We'd had a lot of hiccups with wedding venues, due to either bad luck or filming restrictions, but it all worked out in the end. We were married (again!), surrounded by our closest friends and family, and it was perfect. Besides it being the happiest day of my life with Romain, I also sold our wedding venue that day! *(Photo credit: Tyler Gipe / Gipe Photography)*

Our wedding party, consisting of our closest friends: Alex Becheru, Brett, Jason, my younger sister, Anna, Amanza, and Nicole, who officiated the wedding. Alex isn't on the show, but he owns the company White Glove Estates, which Romain works for as project manager. *(Photo credit: Tyler Gipe / Gipe Photography)*

This is one of my favorite photos of me and Austin, taken at my and Romain's wedding, which was featured on season two of *Selling Sunset*. Austin and my father both walked me down the aisle. *(Photo credit: Tyler Gipe / Gipe Photography)*

Romain and I took this photo on a cliff in Malibu. I love it because it captures our fun and loving relationship together. *(Photo credit: Kayla Swayze)*

Amanza and me doing a best friend photo shoot, in 2020, showing off our matching tattoos on our forearms. We call them our prison tats because we were shit-faced when we got them at a random tattoo parlor in NYC. Hers is upside down and both of ours are blurry, in a random green color. It makes for a funny story though! *(Photo credit: Aria Askari)*

In May 2022, with Romain and Austin, when he graduated from the U.S. Air Force boot camp in San Antonio, Texas. I was beaming with pride. That day, I realized how mature, respectful, and manly the Air Force had made my son.

Romain and I living our best life in Bali, on our delayed honeymoon, in December 2022. After filming season six of *Selling Sunset* and dealing with all of the chaos and my overwhelming responsibilities at that time, I needed this trip very much. We were over the moon to finally have the opportunity to get away for two weeks. It was truly magical.

In New York for Fashion Week, in February 2023, with Natasha Graziano (my friend and motivational speaking mentor) and Amanza. This was my first time at NYFW and it was fun, but I was taking it very easy and only committed to a few shows because I was pregnant at the time. *(Photo credit: Babak Rachpoot)*

Excited about launching my handbag capsule line with Hammitt in March 2023! I spent about a year with their design team working on every aspect of each piece to be included. I chose colors, fabrics, and hardware that reflected my taste and style. It was important to me to offer my fans and buyers the best products possible.

Just under three months' pregnant, in March 2023, days before I had a miscarriage. I began showing early and welcomed the signs of our baby growing. It was a shock and beyond devastating when I lost the baby shortly after.

With Jason in the company sprinter, in May 2023, on the way to The Oppenheim Group office in Newport Beach to make a guest appearance on *Selling the OC*.

At Chrishell's house in 2023, with Heather, Chrishell, Emma, and Bre (not pictured), having a girls' day and spending time with Heather's son Tristan and Bre's son, Legendary (not pictured).

Promoting season six of *Selling Sunset* with Romain on *E! News*. It was our first time there, so we were very excited to be featured by such a well-known platform.

A billboard for my *GOSS* magazine cover, in May 2023. The billboard was in a highly visible and epic location on La Cienega Boulevard in West Hollywood. I was so honored that the magazine chose me for their first cover and billboard. I love that it's a publication by women, for women, that's focused on inspiration and empowerment. *(Photo credit: Lindy Lin)*

Romain and me in Italy, in July 2023. We took his parents on the trip as a special surprise so we could spend quality time together, since we live so far apart and are always busy filming and working. I feel so blessed to call Romain's family my family now. I couldn't have asked for better in-laws, and I absolutely adore his sisters and brother too.

8

Mr. Right

One day you're a "nobody" and the next day you're a reality TV star. Clearly this doesn't happen to most people, but it happened to me when renowned producer Adam DiVello saw a picture of The Oppenheim Group agents in the *Hollywood Reporter* magazine and approached Jason about a show. Apparently, Adam said the photo looked like a group of models, rather than a real estate advertisement, and explained that he'd been wanting to do a real estate show but hadn't found the right cast yet.

Of course, *Selling Sunset* didn't actually come to fruition overnight, though it did happen pretty quickly. After speaking to Jason, Adam came into the office to interview and film a bunch of the agents, so he could see if our personalities were strong enough and interesting enough to carry a series. I guess he liked what he saw, because he got back to us a few weeks later to say he wanted to tape a sizzle reel.

At the time, I was still dating Roger, who came to me and said, "I don't want you to do the show with Jason."

I asked, "Why not?"

And he replied, "Because then our private life is going to become public and everyone is going to see how close you and Jason are."

"So you're jealous of Jason?" I questioned. "He's one of my closest friends. You know that. There's nothing for you to be insecure about."

"I'm not insecure," he replied defensively. "It's just embarrassing. You guys are all over each other."

"That's just the way our relationship is, but there's absolutely nothing romantic about it."

"Well, I don't like it." Roger made his feelings clear one more time.

But since my relationship with Roger was already somewhat strained, I chose to ignore his distrustful behavior and go ahead with the sizzle reel anyway. When that was completed, Adam pitched the concept to networks like E! and Bravo, among others, for probably about six months. Unfortunately, they all turned it down. They said they had enough real estate shows and that there wouldn't be enough of a demand for another one. So we assumed that was the end of the road.

Adam had also pitched to Netflix, but there was radio silence on that front. Even though they were our top choice, we hadn't heard back from them, so we figured they weren't going to bite.

Honestly, I wasn't sure how I felt about it all. I definitely thought the show was a cool idea, yet I knew there were risks involved, such as how producers can distort a scene or dialogue by editing it. I wasn't hugely successful by any means, but I was doing much better, and I was afraid I'd come off looking unprofessional to my clients. But the producers can't edit what you don't give them, and I'm always extremely proper when it comes to my job. The rest of the women at The Oppenheim Group who'd been selected shared similar concerns—we were all excited but somewhat reticent about having our lives broadcast on such a public stage. We asked ourselves and each other questions like: Will the show make us look bad? Will it ruin our relationships with clients? And, on the flip side, will it open doors for us that we'd never imagined would be opened? We had no idea what we'd be getting ourselves into.

I was also aware that Jason had a lot of reservations, which gave me pause. He'd worked so hard to build the agency's stellar reputation, and he didn't want anything to jeopardize that.

Christine, on the other hand, didn't have a moment's hesitation. She wanted to be a star, and her real estate career was a distant second to the fame she believed a reality TV show would bring.

All we could do was wait to see if Netflix would express interest. In the meantime, Roger and I split, and I met Jason and Brett in the south of France to try to get over another miserable breakup.

While I was there, I was communicating via WhatsApp with Romain, the new client moving from Paris to LA. Sebastian—a friend of my old boss at Katana (the restaurant I used to bartend at in West Hollywood)—had reached out to me to make the connection a few months earlier. When I was bartending, Sebastian would come in and have a drink a few nights a week, so I knew him pretty well. I was more than happy to help his friend from France who needed a place to live. I jumped right in as the agent.

Romain had issues getting his visa, so moving to LA was a slower process than he'd expected. While he worked to sort everything out, we had a casual back-and-forth, and I would send him listings to get an idea of what he was looking for and what his budget was. The amazing thing is, during the entire time we were texting each other, I never looked at a picture of him. I probably should have paid more attention. I had no clue that there was this gorgeous, amazing man on the other side of our phone exchanges.

Until, finally, I got a text from Romain saying that his visa situation had been sorted out and that he was in LA, ready to find a place to live. Ironically, I was still in France with Jason and Brett, so our initial meeting had to wait a couple of days.

One thing I can say for sure is that I'll *never* forget the first time I laid eyes on Romain. I picked him up at the bakery where he was working to show him around, and when he hopped in my car, I was practically speechless.

All I could say was, "Oh, hi."

And then I just sat there in my tight tan dress, which had a high neck and a peephole at my chest, gaping at the unbelievably handsome man in the passenger seat next to me. I remember thinking I was happy I'd worn such a cute dress with sexy black-and-tan heels that wrapped around my ankles.

"Hi," he replied in his beautiful French accent. "It's so nice to meet you, Mary."

"It's so nice to meet you too," I said as I noticed his massive legs, which looked like two enormous tree trunks.

His muscles were literally popping up everywhere. I was like, *Oh! My! Gosh! Is this guy for real?* Every time I caught another glimpse of him while I was driving, I couldn't believe what I saw. He was a real-life Adonis.

Though what was even more remarkable than his appearance was how nice he was. We started talking as we made our way around LA, and it felt like we'd known each other forever. We were so comfortable and natural, which is odd, because—given my difficult history with men—I'm typically very jumpy and awkward when I'm attracted to someone. Being that comfortable with a man usually means my heart's not skipping a beat, but it was with Romain. The funny thing was that the guy who showed us the first apartment actually thought we were already a couple.

Once I'd shown Romain a few places, I dropped him back at the bakery and went to the office.

As soon as I got there Jason took one look at me and said, "Oh boy. What happened?"

I announced, "I just met the hottest guy in the entire world! I think I'm in love!" My heart was still pounding.

Then Nicole, one of the other agents and my close friend, came over and said, "You're glowing. I want to see a picture."

So I pulled up Romain's photo on social media, which I later found out was a shot from his modeling days in Australia, where he'd lived for a few years. He was super tan and shirtless. Nicole gasped. Jason laughed. They both knew then and there that I'd fallen head over heels for this man I'd only just met.

After that, I took Romain to see a bunch of other places that week, and as the weekend approached, he asked, "Would you like to go out with me?"

I was super excited that he was interested in me, but I was also somewhat hesitant—again, on account of my past experiences with shitty men. Still, I wasn't going to let this gem of a man slip away.

So I responded, "I have plans with some of my close friends. Why don't you join us? You'll really like them, and you can meet some new people here."

He was like, "Cool, I'd love to."

"Great," I said. "We're going to a spot called Catch for dinner."

What I adored about Romain, on that first date, was that he was charming but not pushy. At Catch, he rested his hand gently on my leg at dinner and held my hand while we were walking to a nightclub afterward. He was very subtle—when he touched me, it was respectful, which isn't always the case, especially with younger men.

I didn't actually know quite how young Romain was until that night, when he told me he was twenty-four—which meant I was twelve years older than he was. That really freaked me out. I was like: *Oh my God! Is this legal?!* In my head, I was thinking, *You're twenty-four years old, which is closer to my son's age than mine!* My brain was just spinning. It took me a moment, but I managed to recover from the shock and had a great time.

That night we ended up kissing and hanging out until 1:00 a.m., when he confessed that he had to be at the bakery for work by 3:00 a.m. The poor guy didn't want to say anything at first because he was having so much fun. It was obvious to us—and to everyone else—that there was this huge connection between us, but I wasn't sure if a long-term commitment was going to be viable. I figured I'd find out that he was insecure or lazy or, even worse, a cheater, like so many of the other men I'd been with. Additionally, I had no intention of getting married for a third time. That thought wasn't even remotely on my radar.

But, as it turned out, all of my apprehensions were assuaged as I got to know Romain better. I realized how mature he was and that the age gap didn't really matter to me. I truly believe that age is a number, and if you click with someone, it shouldn't make a difference. I also knew that I loved being around Romain, even though I wasn't sure where it was going to lead.

From the night we met, we were inseparable. He proved to be the most confident, graceful, and hardworking person I know. Plus, all of my friends were as crazy about him as I was, including Jason.

The only issue was that Romain's schedule at the bakery was insane. He worked twenty hours a day. In Europe, being a pastry chef is a highly respected and lucrative art form. But after he came to the United States, he realized that pastry chefs here are often workhorses who aren't paid very well. He quickly decided that he needed to find a new career that would allow him to grow and succeed in the way he wanted to.

It was around this time, at the end of 2017, that Netflix reached out to Jason and said that, after careful consideration, they were interested in picking up *Selling Sunset* for a first season. Initially, I was concerned that this might negatively impact my relationship with Romain and that he'd view it as an opportunity to become famous, but that didn't happen. He was happy to be involved, though not at all awestruck by it. Romain is one of those people who goes with the flow and is grateful for whatever comes his way.

But I couldn't shake my concern that something was going to sabotage our bond. As a result, a few months after we started dating—I was still living with Christine, and Romain had moved in with us temporarily—I started to pull away from him, as a defense mechanism. I'd get annoyed at him for no reason, which, in retrospect, was very unfair. I felt like my skin was crawling, and I was panicking because I was in love with him and I was terrified of being burned again. It was pure fear.

I knew it wasn't a sustainable way to feel, and I didn't see a solution. So I turned to Jason for advice, and he asked me simple questions, like, What did Romain do to make you feel this way? Why are you pissed at him?"

But I didn't have any answers. I just shook my head and replied, "I don't know. I can't pinpoint it."

"Mary, Romain is awesome," Jason said. "And he loves you. Why don't you take a little break? Go away for a few days and clear your head."

It was an excellent idea—a little space, to think about what I wanted and how I felt, was exactly what I needed.

When I told Romain, he was so sweet. He looked me in the eyes and said, "Please don't go. We're good. I promise."

But I had to do it, for myself. So I said, "I'm just leaving for a couple days. I hope you can understand."

And, like the rock he's always been, he replied, "Okay, I love you. And I'll see you when you get back."

I decided to get away to a city called Solvang, which is in Southern California's Santa Ynez Valley. It's best known for its Danish-style architecture and wineries. While I was there, I focused on listening to myself, away from all the noise, which I couldn't do when I was at home. For forty-eight hours, I sat with my own thoughts and asked myself if Romain was actually annoying me or if I was the problem. Ultimately, I realized that Romain was a great guy and that I didn't need to push him away, which I knew in my heart the whole time. When I returned to LA, I was in a completely different headspace, ready to commit myself to Romain, without a single reservation.

By early 2018, Romain was finally able to switch jobs. He started working for Jason, doing construction. He had no experience, but he didn't let that stop him. He put 110 percent into it, as he does with everything. After a month or so he was already making way more money than he'd ever pulled in from the bakery. Jason was so impressed by his dedication and how he wouldn't let anyone around him slack off. If someone tried to leave before cleaning up, he'd drag their ass back in. Jason observed Romain's work ethic and, pretty quickly, helped him get a better job with a different company, where he became a supervisor and kept learning more and honing his skills. This earned him another promotion to project manager.

Finally, everything was going smoothly on the work front, but we were very aware that Romain's work visa was running out, and a couple of weeks later, he received a notice in the mail informing him that he was going to have to leave the country the following Tuesday. We decided to escape to Mexico for a few days to try to delay the inevitable. While we were there, I began looking into a prenup, just in case marriage was our only option. We didn't say a word to anyone.

In my heart, I knew we weren't ready to get married yet. But I also knew I wasn't ready to lose Romain. Thankfully, he was happy to sign a prenup, if the need arose. That's just who Romain is. He would never feel entitled to something that he hadn't earned and would never take advantage of anyone, much less me. He wouldn't be able to respect himself.

With little other choice, I got the prenup, and on the Friday prior to the Tuesday he was going to be deported, we decided to get our marriage license.

We went to Ventura, California, a coastal city just less than two hours northwest of Los Angeles, where it would be easy to both get the license and get married on the spot.

We needed a witness. My first two choices were Jason and Amanza, but they were both unavailable. I turned to Brett Oppenheim next, because he was like a brother to me, but he said no—because Ventura was too far of a drive and he didn't want to ruin his Friday! This is so Brett; God I love him, but when I tell some stories, both he and I laugh about them! Fortunately, my good friend Nicole (who later officiated our actual wedding) was willing to step in.

On March 9, 2018, Romain and I were married in a civil union ceremony at the Ventura Courthouse.

I wore a simple, fitted white dress. Romain looked dashing in a dress shirt and slacks. We signed the papers, said our vows, and then we went out for doughnuts afterward! We had a good laugh about that and said, "Wow, we're really classy."

We told very few people about getting married—I didn't even tell my family. Since we decided to keep it on the down-low, I didn't wear a ring until we were "officially engaged" that summer.

Romain wanted to make sure I had a beautiful ring, and we'd talked about the styles I liked, but he couldn't afford a real diamond, so he bought me a gorgeous cushion-cut moissanite ring, which I loved. I still have it, even though he's since upgraded it three times with actual diamonds.

I finally had to say to him, "I'm happy with what I have, baby. I don't need any more!"

Even though we were secretly already married, the official "engagement" actually took place on camera and aired at the end of season one of *Selling Sunset*, for the whole world to see! The plan was for us to be in bed together when Romain proposed, and the night before, production had suggested I wear lingerie the following morning when they showed up to film us. I thought the request was a little odd, because I didn't actually know Romain was supposed to be proposing, so I resisted initially. But, eventually, when they persisted, I agreed to it, as long as I could have the covers concealing most of my body.

Getting engaged with a production crew watching us was an interesting experience. Yet even though it was anything but private, it was still very sweet and tender.

It was also a relief, because we were finally able to make it public that we were getting married. And the *real* wedding planning could begin!

While my first choice would have been a small beach affair, Romain wanted something bigger for his family. Understandably, since he'd never been married before, his mom, my cherished "Maman Chérie," wanted her son to have a proper wedding. It was extremely important to his whole family that they could watch his nuptials in person, and I was totally on board with that.

Predictably, the planning process was not entirely smooth sailing. As a start, two of our venues fell through. The second time it happened, I actually thought that the show was screwing with me to cause drama, but—sadly—that was not the case.

As luck would have it, one of the house listings I had was a traditional French estate in Los Angeles and also the perfect spot for a wedding, but I was afraid to ask the clients and risk damaging the relationship.

So Jason stepped up and offered to ask for me.

At first I still wasn't sure mixing work and pleasure was appropriate, even if Jason was asking on my behalf. But Jason insisted it was a great idea, and pointed out that it would garner more publicity for the home we were trying to sell, and it would show buyers that it was an excellent setting for big events.

Not only did the client say yes, but I also ended up selling the property on my wedding day—October 12, 2019—nineteen months after our by-the-book wedding at the Ventura Courthouse. Everyone thought I was out of my mind closing a deal on such a big day, but I told the seller, when he allowed us to book it as our venue, that I wouldn't let that get in the way of selling his home!

*O*ur wedding was perfect. There were eighty guests, just our closest friends and family, which still felt intimate and included my *Selling Sunset* costars Chrishell, Heather, and Maya. Romain and I had joint bridesmaids and grooms-men, which consisted of three women—my sister Anna, my closest friends Amanza and Nicole, as well as three men—Jason, Brett, and our good friend (Romain's boss at White Glove Estates) Alex.

My dad and Austin walked me down the aisle, which felt so right, because they're two of the three most important men in my life. Per tradition, I could have asked just my dad, but I was—and still am—so proud of the man Austin has become. I didn't feel like I could pick one over the other. I wanted both of them by my side.

The decor was a simple white-and-green palette, and I wore a long, sleeveless white lace gown by Floravere. Romain, dressed in Sebastian Cruz Couture, looked so handsome. Getting married to Romain continued to feel so right—there were no preceremony jitters or doubts. I was calm, optimistic, and excited for the life we were going to build together, which was refreshing, given the trajectory of most of my other relationships.

The only part of the day I was nervous about was the vow ceremony; I was delivering my vows in French, to honor Romain's parents. I don't speak the language at all, and I'm a slow learner when it comes to foreign languages. Romain's sister Elodie helped me practice the night before our wedding. I wanted to memorize them, but I decided to read them so there would be no mistakes. Thankfully, saying the vows went perfectly, and since Romain and Elodie's parents don't speak English, every-one thought that was such a special touch. Here's an excerpt, in French, along with the English translation:

Moi, Mary, je te choisis Romain d'être mon mari
De t'aimer quand tu me rends folle
Et de toujours me rappeler à quel point
Je suis reconnaissante de t'avoir à mes côtés

I, Mary, choose you, Romain, to be my husband
To love you when you drive me crazy
And always remember how grateful I am
To have you by my side

I also made sure that my dress revealed the tattoo I'd gotten, written in French, before I'd even met Romain, which translates as: "The only things real in life are you, and dreams, and love."

It was kismet, and truly one of the happiest moments of my life.

9

Rising Star

About seven months before Romain and I tied the knot, the first season of *Selling Sunset* premiered on March 21, 2019, with eight episodes featuring me, Jason, Brett, Christine, Chrishell, Maya, and Heather as the main Realtors, in addition to Davina Potratz and Romain in recurring roles.

Even though I'd seen plenty of other reality series, including ones that centered around the real estate industry, it was a very different experience to actually be on a show as a cast member. I had no idea what it was going to be like to put myself out there and have my private life exposed to the world. Nor did I completely understand what the scope of the show was going to be, aside from what the producers told us, which was that it would focus on women in real estate, including (but not limited to) our careers, our friendships, and our romantic relationships.

Even once we'd started filming, I wondered why anyone would want to watch a show about our everyday lives; it just didn't seem that interesting. But what I eventually came to realize, is that the crew films a tremendous amount of footage, so that they can edit it down to the most entertaining thirty to forty minutes.

This is why you'll often hear reality stars say things like "My comment was taken out of context" or "The chronology of my actions wasn't correct." When editors are piecing together a show from hours and hours of footage taken over many months, in order to make it look like everything transpired in a short time, things can definitely be slightly askew. For this reason, among others, we were all somewhat skeptical about how we were going to be portrayed.

Honestly, that first season, we fought the producers on a lot of stuff while we were filming. But Jason was definitely the most outspoken by far. I'm pretty sure he wanted to produce the episodes himself, which is kind of funny in retrospect. He was constantly saying things like, "No, I don't like that. You should do it this way instead." And then the women would jump on the bandwagon and be like, "I'm not willing to do that." Or "I'm not going to say that." We wanted to be super careful about how we presented ourselves for fear that the producers would spin our actions and words to create drama that didn't actually exist. It was an exciting process but simultaneously nail-biting.

The good news is that once we saw the first cut, we were all relieved that the producers and editors hadn't done anything to make us look bad. I remember Adam DiVello explaining, "I can't use what you don't give me. So, at the end of the day, what you say and how you act is up to you."

Along these lines, Christine made her own bed. Some people loved her, some people hated her, but she certainly didn't hold back. She craved attention, whether it was positive or negative, and she did everything in her power to attract it. Christine's main goal was to be the star of the show, whereas the rest of us were perfectly content to be equal parts of an ensemble. With that said, I believe most of us were pretty true to who we are in real life. We may not have shared every single personal detail of our lives, but we were authentically ourselves and as open as we could comfortably be, given that the filming wasn't something we were used to.

Still, I think there was always a lingering concern that something could go wrong. When you dive into a new situation that's unfamiliar and one that you know is going to impact your life in a major way, you have to be somewhat cautious. For example, in my case, I was newly married to Romain, and we weren't even that far along in our relationship. Accordingly, I had the underlying concern that the smallest taste of fame could change things between us.

Back then, none of the other cast members were showing their relationships on camera. Initially, Romain wasn't being paid but was taking time off from work to film, and often they'd ask him to be available at the last minute. So, eventually, since they wanted him on with me, and he couldn't keep skipping out on his job without compensation, they promoted him to full-time. They'd never done that for anyone else's significant other. Of course, Romain is super easygoing and very easy to get along with. Everybody likes Romain. For this reason, it wasn't an issue to have him join the show, for me or anyone else. And even though I was in the spotlight much more than he was, he didn't care. He was never jealous about the attention I received. Quite the opposite, in fact. He was always extremely supportive and grateful. He took the promotion to full-time cast member in stride, as he does everything else.

It's not lost on me that I've worked with some of my significant others in the past, and it hasn't been easy. But Romain and I get along so well; he's my person. We rarely fight. We're in love and we get each other, which makes being together, both personally and professionally, stressless.

Though Romain was fine with my becoming well-known, I had reservations about how my family would handle my being suddenly thrust into the spotlight. Thankfully, everyone was as encouraging as they could be. My dad definitely doesn't understand my public life and would never in a million years want to be part of it, but he still supports me at every turn.

He'll say to me, "Honey, I'm so proud of you. If you're happy, I'm happy. I just don't want to be involved in any of the TV stuff."

And I'm like, "I get it, Dad. I know it's your worst nightmare!"

My mom is also super proud of me, but she does worry because she knows how sensitive I am. And she knows that when I go quiet, I have something on my mind. Just the other day she called me and asked, "Are you okay, honey? I haven't heard from you in a little while. What's going on?"

I said, "I'm okay. I'm just trying to work through some things and process them in my head."

She was silent for a moment and then added, "I know you always absorb everybody's feelings and opinions. Remember to take it easy on yourself."

My mom is right. I do tend to take on the issues and emotions of my friends, colleagues, and even strangers online, which can be a heavy burden at times. This is why I do my best not to look at social media—I'll read ninety-nine affirmative comments and then one that's really hurtful, and that's the thing I dwell on. Sometimes, it ruins my day. It's hard not to zero in on the negativity.

Honestly, what bothers me most, and the only time I'll ever respond to social media trolls, is when they throw punches at Romain, especially because what they say is so polar opposite of his character. People have called him a gold digger, said I was old enough to be his grandmother, and questioned why he would ever want to be with me, if not for my money. They've also claimed that he doesn't have a job, which is ridiculous. Romain works harder than anyone I know.

So when people attack him for no good reason and with nothing to back up their assertions and assumptions, that makes me mad. Fortunately, over the past few years, most people have become supportive of our relationship, but in the beginning, there were a lot of cruel comments from viewers.

I used to go to him really upset and say, "I'm so sorry, baby. I can't believe these idiots are saying all these horrible things about you that aren't true."

And Romain would just shrug and reply, "Fuck them, I don't care. They don't know me, and they don't know us."

It's so refreshing to be with a man who knows who he is and doesn't let silly stuff like that bother him. I wish I were able to have the same blasé response. What's crazy is that I used to spend hours drafting long messages to the haters. I tried to kill them with kindness while also making sure they took responsibility for their behavior and felt embarrassed by the way they were acting and about what they'd said. I was just so pissed that they were talking poorly about my man. But nowadays I don't reply to any pessimism. I don't have time for that level of negativity, and I've learned how to better handle it. If I do happen to see something mean, I just delete it and block the person. I've also hired a social media team to shield me from the trolls so that I don't internalize everything.

Rationally, I know it's all just projection. People who have that much time to hate are the same people who watch the show and pick apart everything Romain and I do. They're obviously unhappy in their own lives, which is a reflection on them and not on us, but of course it's still not fun to read, and it doesn't feel good. I often have to remind myself of that. I don't need that toxicity in my life and have had quite enough of it.

The other thing people love to go after—specifically with me and the other women on the show—is how we look. They'll comment on my posts or message me directly and say things like, "Stop getting fillers. You look so plastic." And I want to write back (but don't), "I just put on some weight and my face is fuller. I didn't get fillers!" But, again, I know it's better not to engage. I'm not going to lie, though. I have had minimal filler injections in my temples and cheeks and a small amount in my lips from a few years back. I'm not embarrassed by it.

We are our own worst critics, so if a man or woman feels more confident with a little filler or nip/tuck, I fully support it!

How I react to criticism often depends on what's going on in my life and what my emotional state is at the time. If I just got a great listing at work and Romain and I are getting along really well, I let things roll off my back much more easily. I don't even pay attention to the haters. What they're saying is rude, and I don't like or condone it, but it doesn't affect me in the same way when I feel at peace. On the other hand, if I'm already upset about something, the negativity will really bother me. It's like a dagger. So if I'm upset, it's not the actual things the trolls are saying that bothers me—it's the feeling of being kicked while you're down. Fortunately, even with everything I've gone through in my life, I've never been depressed. It's just not who I am.

No one is perfect. Everyone hurts. Everyone has issues. It's hard to understand why people don't get that I'm human just like they are. Just because I'm on a television show doesn't mean I'm emotionless, nor are my castmates.

I don't think I've ever succumbed to the pressure to change how I look based on what other people are saying about me. I get simple age-defying procedures based on how I feel when I view myself in the mirror. I'm very open about what I've had done. I tried fillers for the first time recently, though—as I said—I've been accused of filling my face many times. I've done little things to help with the wrinkles on my neck, because I think your neck can really show your age (so can your hands!), and many people make the mistake of concentrating only on their face. That's really it. I'm in my early forties, and I think I look pretty good for my age. I have nothing to be ashamed of.

My being on television doesn't impact how I maintain my appearance. I'd want to feel confident in myself regardless. Though I will admit that there's a greater pressure to appear perfect. But when my castmates and I do have any simple beauty treatments, we're attacked for looking fake. It's a lose-lose proposition. The truth is, I'm aging; we're all aging. Why is that not allowed? My only goal is to look like a slightly younger version of myself now. I've seen people take it way too far, which is much worse than having a few wrinkles.

I actually don't even know how to edit my own photos. My friends edit everything and laugh at me, because I'll just snap a picture and post it on the spot. I'll admit that sometimes I put a little filter on it, but I feel like that's enough. I mean, how did we live before the Honey filter?!

Regardless, when people criticize my appearance, it does bother me. I have this constant inward battle, which is, on the one hand, to say, *Screw it. I'm over forty years old. I think I look pretty good. If I want to do something that makes me feel better, and you don't like it, tough shit. You don't have to agree, but this is what I'm doing for myself.* On the flip side, I often take what they're saying to heart and think: *Well, I don't want to look fake. I just want to look like the younger version of me. I want to turn back the clock a couple of years, as do so many women (and men).*

Imagine going out to dinner and eating a big meal, posting a photo, and then receiving a thousand comments insinuating you're either overweight or pregnant. Things like: "Look at her bump!" or "You should run to a gym . . . fast." If I'm not too fat, then I'm too skinny. I can never be perfect. Can anyone?

Of course, I get that this is the price of broadcasting my life on reality television, but I don't think that makes it fair.

Even though I'm sensitive, I feel like I'm a pretty strong person overall, and, rationally, I know these insults don't really matter. When I take a step back, I am able to think logically about it. But for so many young women and men, this is not the case. One of my biggest goals is to use my platform to spread awareness about social media bullying. One critical or nasty comment can really destroy someone's confidence. At the very least, words can wound people or even teach them that it's okay to treat other people unkindly. In a worst-case scenario, it could cause people to hurt themselves or even to take their own lives, certainly when the bullying is systematic. To me, that's not only horrifying but also has to be stopped. And now that I have a voice heard by a lot of people, I want to fight against the brutality. I feel like it's my responsibility.

Women get it way worse than men most of the time. The sad thing is that I believe this is because women are the nastiest to other women, and most of the really disgusting hate "mail" that I get is from them, whereas Romain mainly has women who throw themselves at him. Of course, he doesn't pay any attention to them. He's always like, "If you're following me, I think you know I'm married. Fuck off." It's amazing to me how he can just address it head-on and then forget about it.

The ladies on *Selling Sunset* get blasted every single day, all day. We're attacked for everything we say, everything we do, the way we look, how much we eat, how little we eat; it's vicious. Whereas I intentionally do my best to separate myself from it, many of the women analyze every single comment on their posts. They even look at one another's comments to see what people are saying about everyone. I'm like, "How the hell do you have time for that? I can barely keep up with my own page and comments!" Again, it is part of our job to a certain extent, but if I continued to pay that much attention, I'd be in an insane asylum right now.

Even beyond the world of social media, living in the public spotlight is a double-edged sword. While the show definitely provides me a tremendous amount of visibility as a real estate agent, which—in turn—helps me sell more homes, there are also scenarios when the filming schedule gets in the way of my day-to-day progress. During the first season it wasn't as big a deal, because I wasn't as busy back then with brand collaborations, events, and appearances. I was just working and taping the show. I definitely had to stay organized and strategize carefully about how to schedule things, which was challenging on occasion, but I was able to handle it fairly easily.

Now that we're filming, and I have so much else going on in my world, there are many times when I've lost clients or haven't landed deals because of my other commitments. There simply aren't enough hours in the day to focus on everything I have on my plate, and it really bothers me if something falls to the wayside. When the cameras are following us, it's preferred that we keep our phones off. We're not supposed to be taking calls when we're in the middle of a scene that will distract from the main topic and cause any production delays. And if clients can't reach me for hours, they typically feel ignored, which is the exact opposite of what I want. For example, a buyer might call me while I'm taping and leave a voicemail saying, "I can't make it to the showing at two o'clock, can we do it at four or five instead?" Under normal circumstances, I'd pick up the phone and say,

"Yes, no problem." But if I miss the call and can't return it in a timely fashion, they often move on.

After the first season, I didn't get recognized nearly as much as I do now. Back then I could still go out and live my life under the radar, especially if I was by myself. Sometimes people would stare at me, and I could tell they were trying to figure out how and why they knew me, though mostly they'd keep their distance. But over time, it's gotten way more intense.

The first really outrageous experience I had was when the second season was airing. I was sitting in my car at a stoplight right by the Beverly Center, and two girls were in the car next to mine. Suddenly, they started screaming. I couldn't make out exactly what they were saying, but it was so loud that I thought a pedestrian had been hit by another vehicle. Or that something else horrible had happened. I was looking all around me to find the source of their shrieks, but there was nothing going on. Then I heard them yell, "We love you, Mary!" When I realized that all of this commotion was for me, I was shocked. It's strange when you don't view yourself the way others view you. To me, I'm just a simple girl from Indiana. To *Selling Sunset* fans, I'm a reality TV star. It's wild.

And it's only gotten wilder. I'll never forget when the cast was in Las Vegas on New Year's Eve 2021 for a Katy Perry concert. There were so many fans crowded around us that the staff had to guide us to a different section because we were getting bombarded; we literally couldn't take a step forward on our own. Jason and Brett actually had to hide in the bathroom because it was too much for them. Romain and I stayed out there, and we couldn't believe the hysteria.

Fans were running up to us, trying to get selfies, and we were like, "One at a time. Everyone will get a turn." We were trying to be as nice as possible, but it's not easy when people are coming at you. Still, Romain and I stood there for about an hour because we really wanted to make everyone happy. Even though these kinds of experiences can be overwhelming, they're also incredibly flattering, and—for this reason—they don't bother me. I go in prepared. I know I'm there to represent the show; it's my job.

The only time the attention gets to me a little is when I'm attempting to have a quiet dinner and hold a meaningful conversation with Romain or with family and friends, and I can tell that people are gaping at us and trying to overhear what we're saying.

I get asked often if I regret joining the show and if—in hindsight—I'd make the decision to keep my life private. The candid answer is no. I've never regretted it, although at one point I almost quit. After we filmed season six, I said to Romain, "I don't know if I can do this anymore, or maybe I just don't want to do this anymore. There's so much drama going on between all of my castmates, and it's really impacting me." I guess that's what happens when you're so close with the people you work with. I had to ask myself if it was really worth it.

In season seven, I actually resigned from my manager position because of how it was affecting me. I didn't want to be in the middle of all the drama with my coworkers. I'm friends with everyone, and I was in this awkward position of having to manage everybody's personalities in order to keep them from fighting. It sucked.

Not surprisingly, Romain was amazing about it. "You have to do what feels right for you," he told me. "If you want to stay on the show, stay on the show. If you don't, don't. It truly doesn't matter to me. All I care about is that we have each other and that we're happy together. That's our real life."

Throughout all this, speaking to my therapist about everything has been an enormous help. For so many years—when I probably needed it most—I couldn't afford this luxury. Now that I can, I'm absolutely taking advantage of it. I love being able to bounce things off her and get opinions that are completely objective. It was Jason who initially pushed me to see her, because he knows that I take everything to heart and then start questioning myself. She's been such a great sounding board for me.

I actually started going to therapy when Romain and I first got together, not necessarily because of my experience on the show, but because I was having an issue with sex. The trauma of my past made it really hard to be intimate. When I was feeling particularly tense, I had this knee-jerk reaction and would pull away from him, which was understandably confusing and off-putting for him. Therapy helped me realize that my response had nothing to do with Romain but stemmed from, not only the terrible men I've dated, but mostly the rape. It's very important to me that I don't put things on Romain or blame him for things that are the result of residual damage from other relationships.

The therapist I chose specializes in Eye Movement Desensitization and Reprocessing (EMDR), which is a psychotherapy treatment designed to alleviate the distress associated with traumatic memories. Basically, patients briefly focus on their trauma memory while experiencing bilateral stimulation (usually eye movements), which is linked to a reduction in the vividness and emotions associated with the trauma memories.

Immersing myself in this treatment has really facilitated my healing process. It's also helped me believe in my relationship with Romain unconditionally and trust that he truly is the calm, loving, and protective person he appears to be. I know I don't need to worry about him.

It's become an essential part of my life to talk to someone who's a professional not directly involved in my day-to-day. She calls me out on stuff all the time, such as why I'm such a people pleaser. And why I feel guilty about things I shouldn't feel guilty about. She understands me and knows how to talk to me, which is so important when you're looking for the right therapist.

In our sessions, I'm amazed at the things she points out that seem obvious but that never occurred to me. One day, when we were talking about Jeff's death, I told her, "I'm just not good with grief." And she replied, "Mary, if you were good with grief, you'd be a psychopath." Oddly, sometimes it takes someone else to point things like that out to me!

While I don't talk to my therapist about any specifics regarding individual castmates—and I try to stay away from focusing on the show during my sessions—I have discussed the need to put my foot down in certain circumstances. And how to figure out when and if I'm doing the right thing in a given situation. I'll ask, "Am I being overly sensitive?" and "Am I setting boundaries in an appropriate way?"

I find myself telling her stories about how someone treated me and then asking, "Does that sound okay to you?"

And she'll say, "No! That's definitely *not* okay. It's not normal either."

I like that she keeps me in check, because—in my line of work—you can become jaded very quickly.

She'll explain, "It's perfectly reasonable to say no when something doesn't feel right to you, irrespective of what it is. You don't always have to go along for the ride."

Specifically, during season six, with all of the friend drama, there were a number of occasions when I went into her office and confessed, "Sometimes I think I'm going crazy, but then I wonder if maybe they're crazy. I'm so ensconced in it that I can't look at what's going on objectively."

And she replied, "You are not crazy. The situation is crazy. You have to learn to stand up for what you feel is right."

Above all, the most important thing is to stay true to myself. I'd like to think I'm the same me I've always been. And I want to keep it that way.

But it requires commitment and perseverance.

I'm still a work in progress.

10

Friends and Foes

The intersection of fame and friendship is a delicate juncture, especially when the people you work with are the same people you play with. For the cast of *Selling Sunset*, this is very much the case, so during seven seasons it was inevitable there would be a lot of personal drama.

When the show first started in 2019, I was already close with many of my coworkers—though some of us were closer friends than we were with others. I was super tight with Jason and Brett. Heather and I got along really well, and our bond has grown a lot stronger. I had a great deal of respect for Maya and Davina but didn't hang out with them often. And I didn't know Chrishell at all, since she had just joined The Oppenheim Group.

When Christine and I learned the show had a green light and the cameras were about to start rolling, I was excited to have her close by. I still had a few reservations, but it made me feel better to hear how excited Christine was about what was to come. Most nights we sat at home, talking and laughing. Christine is funny, and smart, and was fun to be around. In the mornings she'd make breakfast for us and then we'd go to Starbucks together and chat some more. It was all very normal. But once the show got underway, and the fame piece of our lives kicked in, it became very clear very quickly that the Christine I knew at home was a completely different person from the "character" she played on TV.

In my experience, being on a hit television series brings out different things in different people. Everyone has their own motivations—success, fame, money—which is understandable, but inherent in these motivations is insecurity, which elicits the best and worst in people. For my part, I wasn't in it for the fame; I was along for the ride of an intriguing new experience, with the hope that it would bring both career growth and financial prosperity with it. Yet, suddenly, whatever I (and the other cast members) said or did was no longer just between us; it became fodder for the rest of the world, which led to many erroneous judgments and conclusions. This pressure made certain castmates act unlike themselves. I definitely felt the weight of these negative judgments, though I believe I stayed true to myself in the way I behaved, both in public and behind closed doors, and also in the way I treated those around me.

While I do think that all of us have changed a little bit throughout all the show's seasons—I know I've become more private in my personal life and less trusting of people who want to be my friend—Christine was, without a doubt, the first to display the biggest personality shift. She was very focused on becoming a celebrity. It was as if she were speeding down this track and couldn't apply the brakes. She stopped looking at me, and the rest of us, as her friends and, instead, viewed us as her competition for attention and airtime, things that I never have and never will place value on.

To this day, I don't necessarily fault Christine for losing sight of who she was, and I want to believe it was unintentional. I think everyone on the show has been susceptible to that, living in our weird reality—but at a certain point, you have to own your damaging behavior, and Christine wasn't able to do that.

What was particularly confusing and hurtful was that I thought I knew the friendship we had and the amazing person Christine could be when the cameras weren't rolling. She was always a big personality, and I actually thought her over-the-top antics were funny. But at some point things slipped out of her control—the line between her "character" on the show and the friend I knew blurred. It ultimately drove a wedge not only between me and Christine but also between Christine and just about everyone around her.

I do believe that she legitimately loved and cared for me in the beginning and that she cherished our friendship. I tried for a long time to hold on to that faith and kept trying to make it work, even when I was shocked by the things she did, which included saying damaging things about the show and our producers, maligning Chrishell, and spreading information that wasn't true about other people in the cast. Regardless, I kept fighting and fighting for that friendship until I couldn't tolerate it anymore.

What really stung was our conversation right before she left the show for good, after season five. Production wanted me to have a sit-down with her at a café, outside the office, to see if I could calm her down and get her to stop doing malicious things. At this point, she was still working at The Oppenheim Group, but the atmosphere was very tense when she was around, and we weren't really friends anymore. I was so hurt by how callous she'd become.

I was shaking when I sat down, because I had no idea how she was going to react. I knew I had to watch everything I said, otherwise she'd try to twist my words to make me look bad. As expected, it didn't go well.

I reminded her of how close we once were, but she recently had said to the press: "Mary, we were acquaintances at best. We were never good friends." My mouth had literally fallen open when she'd said that. So I now asked her, "What the hell were you talking about? What have I been doing for the past couple of years? Was I living in an alternate reality? How could I have been so wrong about us? We were roommates. You said I was like a sister, your ride or die!"

And she repeated, "No, we were acquaintances."

Romain was just as surprised as I was. He was there to witness her transformation, as he lived with us for a while, and they had a great relationship too. Christine really liked Romain, and the three of us would hang out all the time. I actually have videos and pictures of them cooking together in our kitchen. We all had a blast together.

I wish I could pinpoint when things changed. All I can say is that it's a tough dichotomy to balance your real life, with people who are true friends, while also working with those same people and being on a television show with them, where all of your issues and interactions are played out in front of a massive audience.

It wasn't easy to put an end to my friendship with her, but I don't regret the decision. For my own self-preservation, I needed to consciously change my thinking to stop remembering and defending who Christine was and, instead, realize who she'd turned into, which wasn't someone I wanted in my life anymore. I still harbor a profound feeling of loss, and it makes me incredibly sad to know that the Christine I knew is gone.

To me, friendship is something to be cherished and nurtured. Because of my midwestern upbringing, and the moral compass that it provided me, I held on to our friendship for too long and was naïve about being able to repair our bond. It was both unexpected and heartbreaking to have a relationship I valued so much fall apart in such a negative way.

When I first moved to LA, one of the most striking things I noticed was how opposite the people were from the folks I grew up with in Indiana. For one, in LA everyone was very savvy and self-serving. And everyone seemed to have an agenda. The attitude appeared to be: I only want to be friends with you if you can do something for me.

In my mind, that's not the way friendship works—it's not supposed to be one-sided—so that was a bit of culture shock, to say the least.

To me, friendship means always having the other person's back, being honest with each other, and going above and beyond to help each other whenever you can. It's also about giving someone the benefit of the doubt because you understand their heart.

When I think about my relationship with Christine, I always find it helpful to compare it to my relationship with Amanza, which has spanned twenty-plus years, on and off. There have been occasions when we've had disagreements, been upset with each other, or didn't talk for a short time. We've always worked it out, though, and thankfully we continue to get closer, regardless of all the obstacles and craziness surrounding us. As always, there are at least two sides to every story, and anyone I'm friends with should know that I look out for my people, and I expect the same in return.

I understand that every friendship has ups and downs, and there's often a learning curve. At the end of the day, we all bring our own baggage, expectations, and boundaries. And even though no friendship is perfect all the time, if you value it enough to learn and work through an issue, you can come out the other side stronger than ever.

In the case of Amanza, who's been an unbelievable constant in my life, there were periods when we lost touch for a little while; she's been through a lot and admits that she wrongfully assessed certain circumstances between us. And I've definitely had moments where I've let her down or my life got in the way too. The good news is that, because we love and respect each other, we've always found each other again. We value our friendship enough to fight for it.

One thing I pride myself on is that I'm generally quick to forgive. I may need a minute, but—even if I'm hurt by someone—my instinct is to try to fix it and make things better, as I attempted to do with Christine, to no avail.

I give a lot to my friendships, sometimes to a fault, which is why I've always kept my circle very tight. Now that fame is involved, this has become even more important to me. It's hard to accept new people into my life and decipher whether their interest is in getting to know me as a person or if they want something from me.

For this reason, in many ways, it has been easier to socialize with the other cast members of *Selling Sunset* rather than try to meet new people, even though—as I said—it's created a lot of drama. Unfortunately, I think this stems from jealousy and competition over fame, fortune, attention, and screen time. I do my best to stay outside of the drama, but it's hard to avoid it entirely. For example, I never anticipated the outcome when my good friend Nicole joined the cast. I thought we were all going to hang out and have fun together. Then I got a big surprise. It was revealed while we were filming season six that Nicole addressed an issue she had with Chrishell because she felt Chrishell had wronged her on a deal from many years ago, one that Jason had brought them both onto, but he didn't communicate the specifics properly and here they were years later.

I was confused and surprised by Nicole's reaction and handling of the whole scenario in general, and I decided to tell her this directly. That's just who I am. I try to avoid drama and don't like seeing my friends fight or get upset. If there's a way to fix a problem, I always try to step in and see both points of view. I know that a lot of people can't do that. Most of the time people are very much in their own heads and focused on only their own feelings. I do my best to explain each person's perspective to both friends, but it gets me into trouble sometimes because both parties believe I'm not defending them vehemently enough.

In this case, I was in total shock because the issue exploded out of nowhere, but there are always two sides and then the truth. In this case, maybe two sides plus Jason's side, and *then* the truth. I told Nicole, "I love you, and I always will. I'm warning you that fighting over this could go south, especially it being your very first season on the show. It doesn't need to blow up like this; calm down and acknowledge Chrishell's position as well."

Nicole held firm. "I'm not going to back down. I know what happened and I'm not okay with it."

Nicole is a very smart woman, so she understood what I was saying and why. She also has a strong personality and is stubborn (just like my husband, LOL), which meant that we had to agree to disagree in this particular instance and move on. She knows that I'll always be honest with her and have her back, but that I'll also tell her when I think she's wrong. She is my girl, and I love her strength, tenacity, and work ethic, but in this situation, it was just too much for me with everything else I had on my plate. Jason was leaving town and had put me in charge of literally everything. Meanwhile, I was injecting myself daily with hormones for a second embryo freezing cycle.

Certainly, Chrishell is my friend too, but I didn't want Nicole to feel like I was blindly siding with her. The truth is, Chrishell and I became very close too. When she and Jason linked up romantically in the summer of 2021, I helped keep it under wraps for months until they were ready to share it publicly. And while they were dating, Chrishell and I spent a lot more time together. She knew she could trust me, not only because Jason trusts me but also because I proved to her that I cared about her, independent of her relationship with Jason. I wanted to protect both of them.

Unfortunately, Chrishell and Jason ended up breaking up, and—when that happened—I had to choose between them on certain occasions, like when they each wanted me to attend a specific event with them. Since I'd been so close to Jason for years and he's also my boss, I got less time with Chrishell than I would have liked. Then, when Chrishell started seeing her partner, G Flip, Jason needed my support because he was taking the breakup really hard. Chrishell and I had drifted apart a little bit, not intentionally, but that's just life. Although we loved each other and still do. About a year later, Chrishell told me she was hurt by me not being there for her as much as I could have been during that time.

When she expressed that to me, I completely understood why, but was shocked and unaware I made her feel that way. I'm the first one to apologize when I feel like I did something wrong, even if it was unintentional. One of my downfalls is that I can often be unaware of a friend's hurt if the friend doesn't say anything about it. In this case, I just thought Chrishell was busy with work and with G Flip. I had no idea my trying to support Jason hurt her and would lead to us starting to drift apart. I was in my own world, but I wish I would've known sooner how she was feeling. Just because I wasn't aggressively trying to see her or make plans with her didn't mean I didn't care. I explained this to her when we finally discussed it. Even though I'm someone who doesn't like to go out at night if I can avoid it and am a total homebody, I should have been more proactive in inviting her over and showing her that she was important to me, separate from Jason.

I'm also not someone who calls my friends every day. Some people are so good about checking in—like one of my castmates, Emma Hernan. Emma is amazing; she checks in on me three or four times a week, just to say, "Hey, babe, how are you doing?

Let's catch up." When I've been sick or going through something, she'll text: "Can I bring you anything?" I love how thoughtful and attentive she is. Conversely, unless you tell me otherwise, I'm going to assume everything is good with you. It's just in my nature. With that said, if I do find out that one of my friends needs something, or if, God forbid, there's a tragedy, I'll jump right in, take over, and fix anything that's fixable to save the day.

I'm so grateful for the friendships I have with the women on the show. Heather is one of my close friends. We're both very private and know we can trust each other, so we confide in each other a lot. Plus, Romain and Heather's husband, Tarek, get along super well, so we'll go out to dinner with them or enjoy staycations together.

Bre Tiesi, who was new to *Selling Sunset* in season six, and I have recently become friends. I didn't have many scenes with her to start, but I like her a lot. She's a strong woman who owns who she is and never tries to be someone she's not. She's also very direct, in a good way, and a great mom, which I really respect. I trust her, because she's straightforward and no-bullshit. I think we both understand each other, even if we don't talk and hang out every day.

As soon as season six aired, I reached out to her to see if she was okay and how she was handling everything. I told her that if she ever needs to talk, I'm here for her. I remember how tough it was when my first season came out. It can feel so surreal, and the backlash from viewers can be exceptionally intense. In Bre's case, she's no stranger to the spotlight, not only because of her previous public relationships but also because she is currently involved with her partner/baby daddy, actor Nick Cannon, who's fathered twelve children, including their son. But it's different when you're the one the public is suddenly focused on. Thankfully, she's really strong. Regardless, I wanted her to know that if she ever needs to vent, I'm here to listen.

There is also Chelsea. She's a character; her personality is larger than life. Season eight was interesting for us, as we had some ups and downs, as well as differences of opinions, but we have made an effort to understand each other and our differences. We respect each other despite them, and as we move forward I hope it brings us closer than before.

It's complicated; that's for sure. It's challenging enough to be friends with the people you work with, but when every interaction you have with those people is analyzed by an enormous audience of strangers, that only adds fuel to the fire. This applies to all of us on the cast and puts us on edge more than normal.

Another friend, who's not on the show, is my girl Natasha Graziano. She's a phenomenal motivational speaker, mindset coach, and bestselling author whom I have tremendous respect for. She's also a devoted friend and a beautiful person. Natasha and I met back in 2019 when I was a guest on her podcast, *The Law of Attraction*, and we hit it off immediately. Since then, we've realized that we have similar histories. We've both endured a lot of struggles, from getting out of treacherous situations, to starting over with nothing, to becoming successful and now trying to help others by making a difference in their lives. I find comfort in knowing that we've fought similar battles for the life we have now.

We laugh nonstop when we're together, offstage especially, because we both talk really fast and can be all over the place, yet we still understand each other's way of talking.

Similar to when I compare Amanza and Christine, when I think about the dichotomy between my interactions with Natasha and Christine, I know which connection is healthy and which one was not. And it's hard to think about going back to that place.

After Christine left the show in mid-2022, I truly never expected to hear from her again. But, lo and behold, I was incorrect. About a year later, in the spring of 2023, I received a text from her, completely out of the blue, saying she wanted to tell me she'd just had a dream about me.

What she wrote after that was a super nice note, which—out of respect for her privacy and mine—I won't detail. I will say that it was both astonishing and bewildering. When I first saw her text, I was like, Is that the name I think it is? I was in the middle of getting ready for a photo shoot for *GOSS* magazine, which is a publication by women, for women, that's focused on inspiration and empowerment. I was in the hair-and-makeup chair, and I just sat there and stared at it with my mouth agape.

I didn't want to reply immediately. When it comes to Christine, I've learned to be extremely cautious, and I've been conditioned to think about how she could use my reaction against me.

After serious consideration, I did write back. But I purpose-fully didn't leave the conversation open for a response.

I said something like, "I appreciate your text. I wasn't ex-pecting it but those are really nice words. I hope you're super happy and living your best life."

I've been burned so many times, and I want to believe that people can change. But I've learned the hard way that I also have to protect myself. Who knows? Maybe Christine's had enough of the chaos. A lot has changed in her life—she's married, and a mom—so perhaps she's settled down. Or it's possible she misses our old friendship.

If Christine reaches out again and asks to get together or says she wants to try to rebuild our friendship, I would need time to think about it. I'd definitely have to talk to my therapist about it too! And really weigh the pros and cons.

The thing is, it wouldn't be just about giving her the opportunity to make amends; it would also be opening up an old wound, opening my heart again, and taking down the wall I've built. It would require remarkable effort to get past everything that happened. Whether or not I'm a part of it, I definitely want her to live her best life. I hope she is truly happy, and that she is becoming a better person. But I don't know if I could put myself at risk again by being involved with her. I don't know if that's the smart or healthy move.

For my part, I always treat others as I want to be treated, and I try to put myself in other people's shoes and understand their perspectives. I believe this makes me a loyal friend, a compassionate partner, and a great real estate agent. Unfortunately, this is not how everyone operates.

I think because I've made so many mistakes in my life, and I've been judged from an early age because of my teen pregnancy, I understand that most of the time we don't know exactly why people feel and react a certain way. But it does stem from somewhere. So I always err toward being compassionate, and I expect that in return.

Fertility and Family

The most important part of my life, by far, has always been family—from my idyllic childhood in Indiana, to becoming a mother to my son Austin at age sixteen, to meeting the love of my life, Romain. Even with all the obstacles I've overcome, and there have been many, I know how lucky I am to have the unconditional support of my parents, my son, my sisters, and my husband. Without them, I wouldn't be complete. And complete is very much how I felt when I married Romain and committed to our future together.

Perhaps, for this reason, Romain and I never had a conversation about having kids when we were dating. In fact, our very first discussion about having children was in front of a production crew when we were taping our inaugural scene for season one of *Selling Sunset*. Not the best plan!

The producer said to us, "We'd like to film the two of you talking about next steps, like getting pregnant and having children."

I remember feeling confused by this request, because—in my mind—I had no intention of having another child. So, I replied, "What do you mean?"

Romain looked surprised by my reaction, which was awkward, to say the least, especially in front of other people and on camera.

I said, "Wait, Romain, do you want kids?"

He answered immediately, "Yes." Then he thought for a couple of seconds and added, "I mean, maybe in five or ten years."

My mouth fell open. "How many?"

I was caught totally off guard, especially since I was certain that I'd told Romain I didn't feel like I needed another child. Becoming a mom had been so challenging the first time that I wasn't inspired to repeat history, despite being at a very different place in my life. Though, in retrospect, it was probably more of a statement that I made to Romain in passing, when I was casually complaining about something, rather than an actual dialogue we had together.

He responded, "You know, two or three maybe."

"You're one hundred percent sure?" It came out almost as an accusation.

"Yes, I'm sure," he said, firmly. I felt affronted.

"You do realize that in five or ten years, I'm going to be in my mid to late forties, right? What if I don't want more kids or what if I can't get pregnant?"

He said, "It's okay for now."

"For *now*? Are you kidding? What are we doing here?" I was instantly defensive. I thought he was saying that our relationship was some kind of time filler, and I couldn't believe we were on such different pages.

Romain, always a calming force, however, explained his comments only after we got home that evening. "What I mean is that I recognize that we're not ready now. We need to be settled in our life together. When the time comes, if we *both* want to have kids, we'll try and see what happens. If you decide you definitely don't want more children or we can't have them, we'll cross that bridge. No matter what, I'm happy with you."

I can't say exactly why that was enough for both of us in the moment, but it was. For one, I think we didn't want to argue about it, and—above all—we didn't want to lose each other.

Plus, at the time, we were both very busy at work, and we wanted to own a house and have plenty of money saved before we brought another human being into the world. I was determined that, if we did decide to have a child one day, it would be the complete opposite of the experience I'd had with Austin—where I always felt like I was running all over the place, just trying to make ends meet, and still failing at something, when what I really wanted to do was just be there for my son.

Fortunately, once I got over the shock of finding out that Romain was fully committed to becoming a father, we had a meeting of the minds. And we were able to move forward with confidence, knowing that whatever we elected to do, it would be mutually agreed upon and we'd both be happy.

After that conversation, three years passed in what felt like a minute, even though we experienced lots of major life changes. Romain and I got engaged. We got married. We moved in to a rental house in the Valley, as we wanted to try out that area to see how we liked it. We also worked a lot and went on a few vacations. Basically, we just lived our lives to the fullest.

Then, all of a sudden, I was in my early forties, and though we still weren't ready to have a baby—and didn't think we would be for a couple more years—I was nervous that I was getting older and that my eggs wouldn't be as viable. I needed a backup plan. So Romain and I talked through our options and landed on embryo freezing as the best approach. Since I knew that the process was time-consuming and that I'd have to make frequent trips to the doctor, we decided to do it in 2022, between filming seasons five and six. This way I could devote all my energy to it without feeling like I was being pulled in two different directions. I also wanted to be as relaxed as possible, which isn't typically how I feel when I'm constantly in front of the camera.

Honestly, I didn't know exactly what to expect from embryo cryopreservation, which is the official name. Basically, in layman's terms, I had to have a series of injections that helped increase my egg count, which meant visiting my ob/gyn's office every couple of days so they could take my blood and perform ultrasounds to monitor how things were progressing.

Once my eggs were big enough (it requires delicate attention to make sure they're just right, not too large or too small), they performed a procedure to retrieve them from my body in order to fertilize them with Romain's sperm and ultimately freeze them. The first step after the retrieval was for my eggs to be placed in incubation to see which ones were going to grow. We started with fifteen eggs, which was a lot, and ten of them were the right size. Seven of those ten were mature enough to be fertilized, and three of those seven made it through fertilization. Those three were then sent to the genetics lab to be tested and analyzed.

Unfortunately, a few days later, in a very disappointing turn of events, we found out that the three eggs that had survived most of the process were abnormal. The doctor informed us that I'd need to give my body a few months to recover, and then, if we wanted, we could go through it all again.

It was discouraging for sure. Not just because we'd expected it to be successful, but also because we'd been able to set aside this rare window, which wasn't likely to be available to us for a second round, at least not straightaway. Not to mention that I would have had to go in every month on the first day of my menstrual cycle, to see if I was ready, which was an impossibility, given my travel and work schedule.

Another eight months went by before an opportunity arose for us to give it another go. I told myself, regardless of my other commitments, I was going to make it happen. If I had to explain to production that this was my priority above filming, then so be it. For once, I'd insist that they could schedule around me, rather than the other way around. Of course, as soon as I'd made that resolution and was already enduring the hormone injections, the girls trip I was in charge of planning for the brokerage, which would air during season six—the one where Chrishell and Nicole had their major falling-out—finally fell into place. The only dates that worked for everyone were in the middle of my embryo freezing cycle. I tried to protest and to really put my foot down about not going, but there was no way out of it.

The show was full speed ahead, and even though I had a lot going on, the intensity of the schedule and filming was necessary.

I knew I couldn't back out of the commitment I had made to the producers and my coworkers. I wasn't the only person who had a lot to juggle—and everyone was just trying to do their job. Even though I was frustrated, I understood that I had to put my personal life aside.

The producers offered to try to accommodate my schedule by suggesting I could drive back and forth from Palm Springs to LA in between shooting so I could make my appointments. But because it was nearly three hours each way, I knew it could never work. I appreciated that they were trying to find a solution, but there wasn't a way to do both.

Ultimately, the experience made me realize how little control I had over my schedule. I felt like I was the referee and manager of everybody else's lives, but not my own. By prioritizing everyone else—from offering to lead the trip, to trying to mediate when there was drama, and just the effort of being *on* all the time—I realized I wasn't taking care of myself.

There's so much that the show has given me, and I will always be grateful for it, but this was the first moment I realized how much I was sacrificing. I felt stuck and overwhelmed. It's not that I wanted to leave the show, but I knew I needed to figure out how to achieve some kind of work-life balance.

I never expected I'd one day become a reality TV star. Before being cast on *Selling Sunset* I barely watched any reality shows (I now watch *Love Is Blind* and *Formula 1: Drive to Survive*). I'd seen episodes of various shows here and there and thought they seemed glamorous, but I'd never thought about how the people on the screen were actually feeling or what they were doing after the scene ended or the credits rolled. I never considered that maybe the persona they were presenting on the screen didn't reflect the challenges they were grappling with in their day-to-day personal lives. I knew that my "character" on *Selling Sunset*—that I was the nice, happy one who always stayed away from drama—was only one side of the coin. My "character" wasn't fake, but I knew for sure that none of the viewers had any idea that I was struggling as much as I was.

I didn't know how I would do it, but I made a promise to myself after the trip to Palm Springs that I would try to figure out how to take better care of myself. Even if it meant not raising my hand to go the extra mile at work for the show, or not trying to "keep the peace" when there was drama with the cast. I would find a way to protect my peace, first.

After a few more months, in late fall of 2022, Romain and I revisited our plan to have a child. We calculated that by the time we were able to freeze our embryos again, we'd want to implant one within about a year, since I wasn't getting any younger. I didn't want to be what I deemed to be an "old" mom and I was afraid that the more I aged, the harder it might be for me to carry a healthy baby to term. Thus, we chose to switch gears and start trying the old-fashioned way. For whatever reason, we assumed it would take me a while to get pregnant. And it would be far less expensive and much easier on me physically and mentally, especially because we were also buying a home and moving as all of this was transpiring. It was simply too much to handle at once.

Romain and I were going a mile a minute in every aspect of our lives, so much so that we barely saw each other during the months of November and December, while we attempted to close escrow, move in, and get our new house prepped for the holidays. We were hosting my family for Christmas, right before we were set to leave later that day for our delayed honeymoon in Bali, where we would escape until mid-January. That vacation, we told ourselves, would be the occasion for baby making without any pressure. And I promised myself and Romain that if we got pregnant, I'd take a step back from being manager at The Oppenheim Group, so I could give more of myself to becoming a mom. It wasn't lost on me that if I didn't have time to even freeze embryos, it might be hard to find the time to be a present parent. But this was the one thing I would not compromise on: being a nurturing parent.

*M*iraculously, or so it seemed, two weeks after we returned from Bali, I found out that I was pregnant. The reveal was polar opposite from the first time, when I was fifteen years old, peeing on a stick in the gas station bathroom, with Shelly waiting outside in her Chevy Cavalier.

When we got back from Bali, I realized that my period was late. I thought there was the possibility that traveling overseas had thrown off my body's regular rhythm, but—same as when I was a teenager—I had a strong hunch, which I shared with the production team of *Selling Sunset*. They knew we were trying, so they asked me directly how things were going and—even though I attempt to keep certain aspects of my life private when I can—I couldn't hide this. As I've said, I'm a terrible liar! Naturally, they wanted to capture the entire thing on camera, so they asked me to wait to take the pregnancy test until they could be there.

I said, "Well, then you need to come over now, because I'm going to do it."

They replied, "We can't; we're in the middle of filming other scenes."

I was like, "Are you kidding? You're going to delay us finding out whether or not we're having a baby?! Can't we just re-create the scene?"

They replied with, "Please just wait until the morning."

And, yet again, I relented.

The following day, bright and early, the crew showed up to tape me taking the test.

With my heart racing, I went into the bathroom and did what I had to do.

Sure enough, after allowing the allotted time to pass, the word PREGNANT appeared, clear as day.

What's perhaps most surprising is that I was shocked, even though I suspected it might be the case.

After I got over the initial surprise, I was both overjoyed and terrified all at once. My brain just kept repeating, *Oh my God! Oh my God! Oh my God!*

Romain was so excited too, but he also had this dumb-founded look on his face, which was hilarious, since we were actively trying and hoping that it would happen for us.

In addition to my absolute astonishment, I suddenly became aware that I had cameras on me, recording my reaction, which made me hyperfocused on what I was saying and doing. Although, even with that knowledge, I couldn't stop my mind from racing and thinking about all the planning that needed to be done, starting with building a nursery in our brand-new home.

My first call was to my sister Anna, but she was at work and not picking up. I texted her: "you have to step away and FaceTime me!" The show wanted to capture the reactions of our family on camera as well, which they did. Anna was over the moon for us.

We also tried Romain's parents, but it was about 1:00 a.m. in France. Eventually his sisters answered, and we shared the happy news.

As far as the rest of my family, I wanted to tell my mom in person, since I knew she was visiting in two weeks. I thought it would be fun to surprise her in that way. I intentionally didn't say anything to my dad or Austin; it was important to me to make sure I was further along, in a safe zone before doing that. And I figured I'd tell my older sister, Sarah, at that point too. The fewer people who knew, the easier it would be to keep it under wraps for as long as possible.

The thing is, I'm still terrible at keeping secrets! Nothing has changed on that front. I had to tell Amanza, since she's one of my closest friends, and I assumed that Jason would figure it out pretty quickly. He's able to read me so well. I also had to film that week—the producers wanted to tape Jason showing all of us The Oppenheim Group's new office space, which is next door to our old one, twice the size, and completely spectacular.

The scene required the whole cast—which meant I was totally screwed. There was no way I could keep such a big secret from all of my coworkers, especially since we would all be together.

As soon as I walked into the new office, I saw that my colleagues were spray-painting their initials on the floor where they wanted their desks to be, and I realized that I couldn't be around the fumes. I was so nervous that my face was going to reveal my secret that I felt like I was going to combust. So, to get ahead of it, I decided that the best course of action was to spill the beans and surprise everyone with the exciting news all at once. But I didn't want to do it without Romain.

Luckily, he was down the street working on one of the houses Jason was selling. I called him, told him what I was planning to do, and asked him to come over quickly. He said he'd be there in five minutes.

At the same time, Heather and Bre started talking about building out a nursery in the space, since Bre had just had a baby and Heather was expecting. Naturally, Jason laughed at this suggestion and was like, "I don't think so."

They pushed back a little, saying, "Come on, so many of us have young kids; it'll make things much easier." Again, Jason said, "Nope, sorry." In that moment, Romain arrived, and I decided to seize the opportunity.

I turned to Jason and replied, "I think it's a great idea. We can make it soundproof. It really would make things much easier for Heather, Bre, and me, if we can bring our babies to work."

Jason responded, firmly, "Absolutely not." He totally missed what I was getting at!

So I repeated myself, saying, "I think we *all* want to be able to have our babies here. Are you listening to me?"

He looked at me, totally confused, and said, "Wait, what? Are you saying what I think you're saying?"

I smiled and so did Romain. And Jason ran up to me and gave me a huge hug. Everybody else quickly caught on and was so thrilled.

I warned them, "No one can say a word, though. We just found out and we're not very far along."

They all promised to keep their mouths shut, but they really rallied around us with love and offers to help in any way they could, which felt so special.

I couldn't wait to broadcast our pregnancy publicly. I even forged a partnership with Clearblue, the world's number one selling brand in home pregnancy fertility tests. Together, we were going to share the joyous announcement once I was in the safe zone.

Regrettably, this never happened.

What was supposed to be the happiest time in my life became one of the darkest times, when we found out, around nine weeks, that our baby had stopped growing.

We went in for a follow-up visit with my ob/gyn—since at seven weeks they hadn't been able to hear the heartbeat quite yet—and while we were there, we received the harrowing update.

I'd lost babies before, but Romain had not, and at first, in part because of the language barrier, he didn't understand what was happening. The ultrasound technician just told us to go sit in the waiting room and that the doctor would see us shortly. Because of my former career in radiology, I read the numbers on the screen and saw the proverbial writing on the wall before they gave us any official information. I didn't want to upset Romain prematurely, so I just said, "I think the baby is the same size as it was at our last visit, which isn't good. Let's talk to the doctor."

Finally, after twenty minutes that felt like an eternity, the doctor called us in and explained that we'd lost the baby. Romain and I were devastated and in complete shock.

What's worse is that, immediately following that appointment, we were supposed to film a scene at our house where we showed the ultrasound pictures on camera.

Romain called the producers, told them what had transpired, and said, explicitly, "You are not coming. We need to grieve alone."

Understandably, the producers wanted our emotions to be fresh when we discussed it. They said they'd just have Amanza there and would keep the crew really small so that it didn't feel too intrusive.

I was absolutely paralyzed and had no idea how to respond. It's not easy to be captured on camera when you're in such a vulnerable state. But I guess that's reality television for you. I signed up, for better or worse. And this was definitely worse. Somehow, by the grace of God, we got through it. I sat there, speaking in a robotic tone, entirely numb, while Romain did everything he could to shield me from any more pain.

I will say that I don't regret it, only because it might help other people out there who are experiencing the same kind of agony.

After that, since my body hadn't naturally passed the baby yet, we thought we were going to have to schedule a D&C (dilation and curettage), which refers to the dilation of the cervix and surgical removal of part of the lining of the uterus and/or contents of the uterus by scraping and scooping after a miscarriage. I called the doctor the morning of the D&C because I began to miscarry on my own. I asked her what to do. She said it was up to me, but that it was probably better to come in and get it taken care of sooner rather than later to make sure everything was removed to avoid infection or a septic miscarriage. She also gave me the option of waiting a bit longer, with the knowledge that there was a very small chance of complications if I chose to do that. I didn't care. In that moment I just wanted to be left alone.

Two days later, I had to go present an award and then, a day after that, I had to go to The Oppenheim Group office in Cabo San Lucas to film a scene, which was over the weekend. I knew I was pushing myself unnecessarily, but I was also grateful for any kind of distraction. On Monday morning, back in LA and heading to the season six photoshoot, I woke up freezing and shaking. I had the heat cranked up and a blanket covering me, but I couldn't get warm, even though everyone else was sweating. I assumed that since I'd never really given myself a chance to rest after the miscarriage, my body was rebelling.

I tried my best to continue to work, but I couldn't, so they ended up sending me home from the shoot. I later found out that I had a septic miscarriage, which is when you have a serious infection in your uterus and your condition becomes toxic.

As soon as I got back to my house, I crawled into my bed and fell asleep, from around 4:00 p.m. until 10 a.m. the next morning.

When my assistant arrived, she took one look at me and gasped, "Oh my God, Mary. You're quivering and your eyes are practically rolling back in your head."

"I think I'm just exhausted," I offered, uncertainly.

It was pretty obvious that what was going on was way more than exhaustion, as I was also bleeding, so she called the doctor.

The doctor instructed me to go to the ER immediately, indicating that it was a dire situation. Yet, for some crazy reason, I insisted on going to work first to film a scene, which didn't go well. I knew I had to get to the hospital quickly, for the sake of my health.

Miraculously, I got through filming the scene.

When I arrived at the doctor's and had an ultrasound and bloodwork taken, she said I needed surgery right away to clear the toxic tissue from my uterus. I told her that I had another scene to film with my sister and that I didn't want to disappoint her, so I needed to come back the next day.

The doctor was stunned that I was willing to compromise my own condition for something so seemingly frivolous, but I ignored her concern and begged her to give me an antibiotic, with the promise that I'd return the next morning for the surgery. After protesting multiple times, she finally conceded, against her better judgment.

She said, "I'm giving you the strongest dose of antibiotics. If you feel *anything* out of the ordinary, drop whatever you're doing and come to the hospital instantly." Then she paused, looked at me intently, and added, "I want you to know that I strongly recommend against this."

I nodded and replied, "I understand that, but I have to go do this. I can't let my sister or the show down."

I honestly can't explain why this is the decision I made. I know it sounds irrational. I just hate disappointing people and always believe that I can somehow power through.

Once the surgery was complete, it was time to start the healing process. All I can say is, I thank God for Romain every day. He was beyond supportive. We barely even talked about his feelings because he always was saying, "I'm fine, I'm fine. I just want to make sure you're okay." He was so sensitive to my feelings. If I started crying or even didn't want to talk, he was understanding. He didn't make grand gestures or eloquent statements; he was just there for me, whenever I needed him. And that's what I needed most. I hope everyone will, at some point, have a Romain in their lives. There's truly no better feeling than unconditional love. Losing this baby hit me harder than I'd anticipated. I've never suffered from depression, but I think I got as close as I'll ever get in the few months following the miscarriage and surgery. I know so many, too many, women experience this same kind of loss and heartbreak all the time. I want to be open about my experience in hopes that it can help even one soul suffering from the same thing, so you know you aren't alone and it's not something we as women need to feel ashamed of.

Ultimately, I was diagnosed with a septate uterus (via a full body MRI scan). It's a rare genetic condition in which a septum was formed, giving my uterus a heart shape and making getting pregnant and carrying a baby difficult. With surgery the septum can be removed, though, to increase the likelihood of a successful pregnancy.

I can still carry a baby, but I'll need to undergo a number of tests, including a surgery, to figure out the best approach for future conception.

So, as of now, Romain and I are still very undecided about how we're going to move forward with getting pregnant. In an ideal world, we'd love for it to happen the old-fashioned way, but one of us always seems to be out of town when I'm ovulating. On the flip side, fertility treatments can help but they're a lot to endure, not only for my body, also in scheduling the timing.

I know there are some studies indicating that you're more fertile in the three months after miscarrying, though—as I understand it—the evidence isn't solid enough. Either way, I just wasn't ready; it had taken a major toll on me. We'll make a decision as soon as we can; we have to, I'm not getting any younger.

In the meantime, Romain and I got a fur baby—the most adorable Pomeranian ever, named Thor. He's about four pounds and he's going to stay that small. But he's got a big personality and is such a sweetheart. Romain is obsessed with him. We're both in love with him.

If having a baby isn't in the cards for us, Romain and I are okay with that.

I'm so grateful to have such a resilient and devoted man in my life. He's my rock and the only person I've truly leaned on throughout my entire fertility journey.

Romain and I know how blessed and privileged we are. We don't take that for granted for a single second. And we know that not everyone can have everything they want.

We also understand that the universe works in interesting ways. We're prepared to confront whatever comes to us. Together.

12

Facing Forward

Though having a child together definitely continues to be a priority for Romain and me, we had a very unpleasant distraction recently, which wreaked havoc on our lives and waylaid us from concentrating on anything else. Though we didn't know what it was, it originally surfaced about a year ago, while we were still living in our old house. It began to come to light, for me, when I started seeing these random warnings popping up on my computer. It was something to do with the terminal box—I didn't even know what that was—and I couldn't close them out. So I sent a screenshot to Austin, because he knows a lot about that kind of technical stuff. He said that it didn't make any sense to him and he wasn't sure what it was. It was super annoying and I wanted it to stop, mainly because something about it was making me feel uneasy. For whatever reason, I was scared that someone was watching me. I remember talking to my therapist about it, and she said that perhaps I was just getting used to being in the public eye. That sort of made sense. Maybe I was just being paranoid.

When we moved to our new house, for the first couple of weeks, everything was okay. Then, little by little, I was noticing these subtle—and very strange—things happening on my computer and on my phone. For example, Amanza would come over, I'd say something to her, and then a related item would appear on my computer the following day. It was very subtle but increasingly concerning. Before long, these sorts of things were happening constantly, and I refused to believe it was a coincidence. I couldn't escape the feeling that someone was listening to me and spying on me.

I kept trying to tell Romain about it, but he never saw these strange things because they would always happen after he went to bed for the night. Luckily, I took screenshots of everything. And I started educating myself so I could figure out what the hell was going on. I unplugged all our cameras, our Wi-Fi, and everything else I could disconnect. Romain would wake up and say, "Baby, why did you do this, again?" And I was like, "Baby, I'm sorry. But I'm telling you there's something weird going on." He would reply, "I'm here. Don't be scared. I'll protect you." I was like, "No, you're sleeping when it's happening and you don't believe me." This went on for many months. I thought I was going crazy because I couldn't shake it. I kept asking myself: *Why am I feeling this way? Is this all just my own wariness from being on television?* In my heart I knew it wasn't, but my brain was questioning my heart.

A couple of things happened after that. First, Romain was finally sitting next to me when out of the blue my phone started going haywire. He asked, "What the fuck is going on?" And I said, "I told you!" Both he and my former assistant suggested that I wipe my computer clean and reload everything back onto it, which I did. I also changed my passwords about thirty different times, but neither of those things helped.

Once Romain saw what was going on, we called his friend down in San Diego, who used to be a hacker and who now deals with security systems and firewalls. His friend said he understood what I was saying, but that it probably wasn't as bad as I thought. He explained that, typically, hackers just get in, take your money, and get out before you even know anything is wrong. But I was describing a targeted hack, which was very rare and unlikely. Still, he agreed to drive up and take a look.

When Romain's friend arrived, he immediately looked at both my computer and my phone to see what was going on. He said, "The good news is that you're not crazy. The bad news is that this is way worse than you or I thought it was. Whoever these hackers are, they've downloaded everything. They've been accessing your cameras and your microphones on your computer, your phone, and your security cameras, and they're even sending messages through your thermostat."

I was freaking out. While I knew that there was something fishy going on, I had no idea how serious the violation was. Romain's friend—who sees a lot of high-tech hacking—had never seen anything quite this insane. I had to rewire my entire house, buy a brand-new computer, a brand-new phone, and all-new super professional, high-grade cameras, like what banks and the military use.

The whole process took forever. While it was going on, I actually went to stay in one of Jason's homes and didn't tell anybody where I was. I had to have the tech systems in my car wiped clean as well, because the Apple CarPlay had connected to my phone, so the Porsche I drive could be tracked. These hackers had all of my passwords. They knew where I was at all times. I don't know if they were local or from another country, but—either way—we had to err on the side of caution. It was such a nightmare and an unbelievable invasion of my privacy.

And it definitely was not random. The hackers very specifically targeted me because of my fame. As Romain's friend said, they could have just stolen my money and been done with it, but they didn't touch my money. They just watched me and listened to me for eight straight months. They could hear every word I said, see me getting out of the shower, and witness me going to the bathroom. Just thinking about it makes me feel sick.

It's a truly awful experience not to fully know the scope of what they saw and heard. When I'm not in professional mode—selling houses and attending work events—I barely leave my house. Wherever I'm living at any given time is my sanctuary, and they ruined that for me. They robbed me of the ability to feel safe in my own space. I remember walking from room to room, crying, and thinking: *I don't know where to go.* It was so invasive, especially for someone like me, who values solitude and confidentiality above most things in life. Honestly, I'd rather have had someone break into our home and point a gun at my head. At least, in that case, I would have been aware of the threat and had a chance to fight back. My therapist said it sounded like the worst kind voyeurism, where the person gets off on knowing everything about you. They weren't just hackers; they were stalkers too.

Thank God they didn't do anything to hurt me, physically or publicly. They just fucked with me in a major way. We still don't know who it was, and we may never know.

Because of our continuing concern, we also installed a new security system that is supposed to be airtight. That lets me sleep at night, though my guard is still up. How could it not be? Once you've been taken advantage of like that, you're hyperaware. Believe me, it's not the way I want to live, but I was given no choice. It's one example of the ugly side of being a celebrity. People want access to you. And when they can't have it, they find a means of getting to you without you knowing.

The only positive result of this horrible experience is that it led me to discover a great product that I now use—a special privacy case for cell phones. But I hope to manufacture my own improved version of it. As I mentioned, I've been looking to expand my brand. And though I'm still focusing on the many areas I love—fashion, cosmetics, self-care (more to come later in this chapter)—technology is now on my radar too! Because of what happened, this new venture is entirely organic and is, without a doubt, the right fit for me.

Now that we've overcome this hurdle and I'm planning to turn lemons into lemonade, I've refocused my energy on growing my career.

Workwise, the real estate market isn't great; it's been really slow in fact. But I have some solid prospects on the horizon. Currently, I have another listing from a repeat client for $28.5 million, which is amazing. I'm also working with six additional clients—2024 is going to be an epic year, I can feel it!

And *Selling Sunset* continues to be a huge part of my life—after the eighth season airs, it will be the longest-running series on Netflix to date.

Thankfully, we have so many diehard fans, and we seem to be accumulating more. Recently, I walked outside the office to get a breath of fresh air and a woman was standing there, crying hysterically, because she's obsessed with the show and couldn't believe that she'd gotten to meet some of us. Such devotion keeps me optimistic that we'll be on the air for a while. And I plan to remain part of it as long as my mental state can handle the pressure and my body can endure the long hours and constant stress.

With that said, I'm well aware that fame can be fleeting. One day the show could be on top, and the next day it could be canceled. It's especially risky in our case, because the cast is constantly evolving, and it's impossible to predict who will resonate with viewers and who will not. Also, some of the veteran cast members are burning out. Being on a successful series can be very rewarding, but it's definitely not easy. It's a massive commitment and a lot of hard work. The success of the show has given me so many other opportunities that are significantly less demanding than being part of the cast—like brand partnerships and speaking engagements, both of which I'm pursuing.

A recent collaboration I'm really proud of was with an amazing handbag company called Hammitt, which was conceived in 2008 by a small team of Californians who wanted to build a client-focused company where form meets function and only quality, long-lasting materials are used. Since I'm extremely passionate about the purses I carry, this one was a natural fit. I hadn't heard of this particular brand until they sent me one of their bags—a big perk of being a reality TV star—but once I'd received it, I fell in love and couldn't live without it. Immediately, I bought a couple more of them and started talking to the folks at Hammitt about partnering. Ultimately, I met their executive team and told them I'd relish the chance to design a bag with them. I've always been very into fashion and design, so it seemed like a natural next step. Additionally, since I have so many bags, which often have to go from day to night, I know exactly what I like in the way of look and performance.

For example, I adore the appearance of white bags, but in my line of work, they're virtually impossible, since I'm always getting spray tans and having my makeup done. There are so many details to think about when designing, and I was very thoughtful and particular about my decisions. With Hammitt's prototypes as my starting point, I picked all of the details to complement them—everything from the pattern of leather and the interior material to the interior color, the pockets, the handle, and the hardware. There were a few features that they said would be too challenging to construct or too pricey, but I insisted. When something is important to me, I hold my ground. As a consumer, I felt I knew what other consumers would be drawn to, and I was right.

Hammitt x Mary, The Sunset Collection celebrated all things luxury and sold out in the presale stage. We're currently in talks to produce a second collection.

It's been such a wonderful experience for me. I loved being able to exercise my creativity, and it was so rewarding to create a product from start to finish. Plus, I got an inside look at an entirely different industry. (I thought I knew everything about purses, but there was still a lot to learn.)

Another partnership I did, which made sense for me, was with the company Nutrafol, which makes clinically proven supplements that target thinning hair. What I really appreciate about Nutrafol is that it's 100 percent drug-free and formulated by a physician to help hair look visibly thicker and grow faster. Because I get my hair done professionally for the show—sometimes multiple times a day—and also for events and appearances, it's often completely fried. When my hair was styled in a shorter bob and platinum blond, it was extra damaged. And people were so cruel about it on social media. They said I looked disgusting and that I was going bald. The trolls even went so far as to suggest that my hair was falling out because I was on drugs. I was really shocked. So when Nutrafol reached out, I did my research and agreed to collaborate.

Xifaxan, which treats irritable bowel syndrome, is another partnership I'm proud of because I suffer from the condition and it can control my life. I'm beyond grateful that this medication actually works and my symptoms have dramatically improved. I'm also the poster child for ADHD! Not sexy, I know, but I'm determined to raise awareness, which will help diminish any stigma associated with these conditions.

I know there are a lot of celebrities who will partner with almost any brand, purely for the paycheck. But that's not how I roll. I always try the products first and make sure there's not some kind of scam going on. If I represent and recommend something, and other people then end up having a bad experience with it, I know that my endorsement of a product will be useless in the future. I wouldn't trust someone who told me to buy something that didn't work, no matter who they were.

For me to attach my name to a product, whether it's a purse or a beauty item, it has to feel organic and unforced—I won't succumb to the pressure to represent something just for the money. Occasionally, I'll even lower my fee if it's something I feel strongly about having made a difference in the way I look or feel.

Fortunately, I do currently have someone who can negotiate my deals for me; however, I still make all of the final decisions myself. My business managers pitch me the stuff they think I'll like and present those offers to me. I then study the brands, get a sense of what the deliverables will be, and figure out how I want to proceed.

There are plenty of times when a deal simply doesn't work out, for one reason or another. For instance, I was in talks with two companies—one that specialized in skin care and one that was dedicated to fragrance. The issue in the first case was the exorbitant price of producing the item, and with the other, it was their remarkably slow response time. I kept trying to get business done and move things along, but they were operating at a snail's pace. I wasn't willing to ruin my reputation in either situation.

This doesn't mean I won't get into skin care eventually. I believe I will, because it's a true obsession of mine. I literally have to control myself every single morning and night, so that I don't pile on a million different creams and serums! I have to stick with a strict routine to avoid breakouts. I know the right skin care prospect will come to me. Timing is everything.

As I've gotten older and the show is heading into new seasons, I've started to try using my platform more intentionally by taking on more speaking engagements. The demographic I present to is mostly women between the ages of twenty and sixty, because my focus is female empowerment, but men do come as well, and they seem to be just as motivated by learning how to grow their careers, how to overcome obstacles, and even how to treat other people along the way. But it's women, unfortunately, who often put down other women the most. There's this inherent competition that can turn into a bullying of sorts, where we're actually mean to one another. I don't engage in this kind of behavior, but many do. On the flip side, men are typically better at staying in their own lanes and keeping their eyes on the prize, without worrying about what's going on around them.

I'll never forget my first speaking engagement. Before it, I wasn't nervous at all. I thought, *I've got this*. I just have to get up there and talk about my life and my experiences. How difficult can that be? Then I realized I was going to be addressing roughly three hundred people with a keynote speech. And that I was also participating in three panel discussions, which is a lot!

To make things even more challenging, I had COVID right before the event, and I felt like complete crap. On the one hand, I was super grateful that I'd tested negative the day prior and was able to get out of quarantine at the eleventh hour, as I hate backing out of commitments. But I was still extremely fatigued and hadn't had the time or energy to prepare, as I usually would, ahead of time.

On the way there, I started freaking out. I was like, oh shit, I have to tell my story in a straight line without allowing my ADHD to take me on all kinds of tangents. I'd made some notes and bullet points on my phone to try to keep myself on track, but when I got up onstage, I couldn't hold my phone because my hands were trembling so badly!

By some leap of faith, I was able to pull myself together. I looked out into the audience, at the sea of eager, smiling faces, and it energized me to be my best self, even though I was feeling under the weather.

Once it was over, I had to sit down and take a minute to just breathe. I was still shaking from all of the adrenaline, and I feared I might pass out or collapse from fatigue, but I was also really proud of myself.

The most rewarding part of giving this speech was that people were coming up to me afterward, telling me how inspiring I was and sharing their own stories. They said they had no idea I'd been through so much and shared that the life lessons I'd imparted made a big impact on them.

For me, that's the whole point of doing these speeches. So even though it was a bit of an out-of-body experience and I was worried that I was just up there rambling, in the end I achieved exactly what I wanted, which was to make people think about how they can change their lives for the better.

Since then, I do these types of engagements every couple of months, and I definitely feel like I'm helping people. I talk about my life—the many hurdles I've cleared to get where I am today—and I do my best to motivate people to chase their dreams. I explain that I wasn't born into success or the limelight. I struggled for decades, as a single mom, to reach my goals. I tell anyone who will listen that if they think they'll never accomplish what they're striving for, they can and they will. It requires hard work, perseverance, and learning from your missteps. You have to involve yourself with smart individuals and be confident in your own instincts. If your gut is indicating that something isn't right, it probably isn't.

Something I'm planning to add to my speaking engagements is a section on social media bullying. It's an issue I deal with so regularly in my own life, and it's becoming more and more rampant every day, especially among vulnerable adolescents. At this point, I'm grateful to know who I am and that I'm resilient enough to handle the abuse—most of the time. But all the teenagers and younger kids who are still trying to figure out who they are, and are constantly being told they're ugly or fat, are being torn down by cyberbullies. It's so important to show empathy for others, even if you don't know them personally. It can be challenging to truly understand what someone else is going through, which means you have to consider this in the way you treat not only your friends but also complete strangers.

When people aren't treated with compassion and kindness, the result may not be simply a bruised ego or hurt feelings; cruel comments can lead to severe anxiety, depression, and even suicide. It's heartbreaking, and my mission is to do everything in my power to put an end to it. I want to lead by example and wake people up to this abhorrent behavior.

A big part of the solution, in my opinion, is changing your perspective. Rather than being jealous and angry about someone else's situation versus your own, I want to shift the concentration to motivation. When you see someone on Instagram who's succeeding, instead of throwing stones, ask yourself, What are they doing correctly? And then say, I'm going to do that too.

I plan on devoting a lot of time to public-speaking engagements, and using my platform to advocate for women everywhere. My heart has always been deeply connected to the world of women's health, and I want to make a difference. From the whirlwind of early motherhood to navigating the complexities of fertility struggles, my journey echoes the highs and lows experienced by so many. I have such deep empathy and know all too well how difficult and lonely these health issues can be.

Because of recent complications with my own health, this subject has become even more personal and important to me. After receiving a full-body MRI for preventive health care, I discovered that I had a ruptured breast implant, as well as a few concerning findings related to my fertility. These results pushed me to make my health an even bigger priority, and use my voice to encourage other women to do the same.

I had no idea that I had this rupture, and it could have been very dangerous had it been left unattended. Women naturally wear many hats and often take care of everything else while putting their own needs to the side, but I want women everywhere to have the tools, access, and awareness to prioritize their health. It's not just about championing a cause; it's about bringing awareness with commitment and understanding.

With this goal in mind, I recently had the honor of joining the American Association of Gynecologic Laparoscopists (AAGL) Board of Directors. I'm hopeful that this will give me an opportunity to make a difference far beyond my social media platform. The AAGL provides opportunities for education, mentorship, global outreach, and patient advocacy, with the ultimate goal of improving women's health.

Every woman deserves the spotlight in matters of medical care, and I'm dedicated to ensuring that the necessary resources and attention are at the forefront.

This isn't just a personal chapter; it's an opportunity for me to use my platform to help women globally. My vision is to elevate accessibility to health care, creating opportunities for women to prioritize their well-being with true compassion and community.

I'm more inspired than ever to use my influence to do good in this world. I don't know if I'll be on television forever, so now is the time. It's hard to imagine what life will be like when my time on *Selling Sunset* is over. Although Romain and I have discussed doing a spin-off, if and when the show ends. We'd love to do a show where we renovate and flip homes and also travel the globe—two of our passions.

When I look at how far I've come—from my childhood in Indiana, to a teen pregnancy, to raising an amazing son while enduring a handful of toxic relationships, and finally meeting friends who've become family, along with the love of my life—I feel a lot of pride in how much I've evolved as a human being and how successful I am today, both personally and professionally.

I'm definitely stronger and more resilient than I've ever been. When I look back at how I used to communicate, especially with someone like Drew, I realize that I'd never take that shit now. I'm still very careful about how I treat people, because I never want to hurt anyone. But I will never again diminish myself if it threatens my own sanity and well-being. I've come to understand that when someone mistreats me, it's not my job to make them feel better about what they've done. That's on them. I can't mother people in that way anymore. I do still find myself putting others' needs in front of my own, and I'm trying to work on that, but I don't want to change that too much, because I think it's a nice part of who I am. I just have to be better about taking care of myself and honoring my own values.

My life has hardly been a linear journey. There were so many times when I let the fear of ruffling feathers or instigating conflict get in the way of standing up for myself. One of the things

I'm most proud of is the way I've learned to advocate for myself. When I think about teenage Mary, or who I was with Drew, or even as recently as the person I was on the first few seasons of *Selling Sunset*, I see a young woman who knew what was right and what was wrong, but couldn't always find her voice. I was so worried about disappointing or upsetting people that the idea of prioritizing my boundaries or what was best for me felt impossible—a lot of times, it wasn't even an option on the table.

I think a big part of being able to find my voice was going through those experiences, sometimes learning things the hard way, and finally figuring out that I was my best advocate. Looking back, I'm not ashamed of who I was, and don't regret any of the decisions I've made, because I know that each trial taught me something different. And thanks to each challenge, I feel so much stronger now—not in a hardened way, but with a kind of quiet confidence and resilience that makes it easier to speak up for myself, maintain healthy boundaries, and focus on what's actually important.

And with Romain by my side, that confidence feels super charged. Being in a healthy relationship with the man I love, and who I know will always be in my corner, makes the tough moments feel manageable. I feel so grateful that I can share my life with a partner who makes me feel like the best, strongest version of myself. After a long day at work or filming or anything else, coming home to Romain is exactly what I need.

There's so much I want to say to my younger self—the scared fifteen-year-old who just found out she was pregnant and had no idea what her life would be like. So, I wrote a letter

to myself, to express all the things I wish I could have known
back then:

Dear Mary,

I'm going to start this by saying that you made
the right decision to follow through with the
pregnancy; don't second-guess yourself because
of the gossip and how difficult life seems at
times. I know you want and need a break, but
I promise this phase of life will mold your
character in a way that you can't imagine right
now, but that you'll come to understand in the
future. Keep pushing forward and don't lose
hope, keep being kind and optimistic; this is simply
bootcamp to prepare you for what's yet to come.

I know how hard and deeply you love, so please
allow me to save you some heartache, but you
must listen closely when I say this. Take your time
when you feel like jumping into a relationship,
people are not always what they seem, and it
takes a long time to figure this out.

Time passes too fast, so enjoy each moment to
its fullest. Take it all in, because you won't get
those moments back.

When you lose your way and make mistakes,
remember your core morals and values. These will
keep you afloat in times of despair.

Be very selective about the people you
surround yourself with and trust. I pray you will

be able to avoid negative situations; however, if you can't, please remember that there's always a lesson to be learned. People will deceive you, and they will burn you, often when you least expect it. As you move forward, the valuable wisdom you take away from these moments and events will prompt you to begin to protect yourself more by keeping your circle close and small. That will work well for you in life. There's nothing better than knowing who you can count on.

This doesn't mean you should be scared to take chances. Sometimes people will surprise you in a positive way too.

Travel as much as you can; it will open your mind and make you a better human. Remember your central values and treat others as you would want to be treated; it will serve you well.

Trust your gut instincts in times of crisis; you have incredible intuition, and one day you'll change the outcomes of people's lives if you trust your inner compass. Be sure to focus on setting boundaries; this will be a tough one for you because you'll want to say yes to everything and everyone, because you love to help people. Unfortunately, you'll come to realize that not everyone can be helped. It's simply not possible, so practice saying no when necessary. And practice being able to walk away without looking back, when there's nothing left for you to do.

Appreciate your family—they will be your closest friends and constant supporters throughout your life. Your mom, your dad, your sisters, and your son, Austin, are everything (yes, you're having a boy, and that's his name).

You will find true love. I promise you that. But it will take time, and you will meet the wrong men along the way. Still love will come to you when you least expect it.

You will be happy.

You will be strong.

You will overcome every obstacle in your way.

You will be you, through and through, and that will be enough.

Love Always,

Mary

Sometimes when I'm in the backyard of our beautiful new home in Toluca Lake, attending to my little herb garden, I turn around and look at my house, and I can't help but pause and take a moment to revel in what I was able to make happen, especially after everything I've been through. Or when I'm on the red carpet, I'll absorb my surroundings—the flashing lights, the crowds, the spectacle of it all—and think, *How the hell did I get here?* It's pretty unbelievable, even to me. I don't know if it will ever fully sink in or if I'll ever get used to it. I hope I'll always remain humble. It's who I am and who I've always been. Even though everything in my life is so different from what I'd ever imagined, and I've changed in so many ways, there are a lot of things about me that remain constant. Keeping my feet on the ground is one of those things, and my relentless optimism is another.

Facing life's challenges with a smile isn't easy, but I don't think I would have been able to make it to where I am today without consistently trying to find the bright side of things. I can't wait to see what the future holds. I'm ready to embrace every enticing opportunity that comes my way. And to grow my career and my family with Romain. In the meantime, I'll just keep doing my thing. And, as always, I'll continue Selling Sunshine.

ACKNOWLEDGMENTS

There are so many people who helped make this book a reality and who support me every day. I'll start with my husband and family.

Romain, you are the most beautiful soul both inside and out. Your integrity, loyalty, dedication, and consistent positivity took me by surprise. Thank you for being you, and for loving me. I'm so blessed to have you as my husband, my best friend, and soulmate. I love you more every day; you are my rock. You make every day entertaining and my heart 100 percent complete.

Austin, I learned at a very young age to overcome any hurdles life throws us to give you a better life. I've made mistakes without question. Thank you for being patient with me while I figured it all out. You are the biggest gift and accomplishment of my life.

Mom, thank you for all that you've done. You have shown over and over what a mother's love truly is. Your heart and your love for your family represent true selflessness. You have always been there for me, and you've pushed me to be better, by making me take ownership of my mistakes, which has helped me become a strong woman. I wouldn't be here without you; thank you for your unconditional love and sacrifices. You're the best mother I could hope for, and I'm beyond grateful to have you in my life, not only as my mom, but also now as my friend.

Dad, you mean more to me than you'll ever know. I'm not sure I can find the words to properly express how much I love you and what you truly mean to me. I've been so blessed to have you as a father and role model, showing me patience and unconditional love throughout life's ups and downs. Thank you for everything you've done for me and what you've taught me along the way; thank you for giving me the best childhood I could dream of and instilling in me the morals and values that I still honor. Hopefully I can use those morals and values to help make the world a little better one day. You are my hero. I love you, Dad.

Anna, you are the strongest person I know; you are my ride or die and my confidante. I love you, sissy-poo! You've been through it all with me and prove to me every day, by example, that no matter how hard things get, there is a beautiful day just waiting for us if we power through. I'm so proud of everything you've accomplished. I'm in awe of your internal strength, your dedication, and your gorgeous soul.

Sarah, my beautiful and selfless older sister; I look up to you so much. You have consistently been a rock for your family, putting them first through tough times, and you've done it with grace and a smile. You are an inspiration to me. I love you so much and am so grateful for the memories of childhood experiences we had together. From cruising Applewood as teens, to the Garth Brooks concert with Anna and me sick in the back seat of Steve's car (whoops!), to us drinking on the kitchen floor after his funeral . . . no matter how many miles are between us, this bond and love we have will never be broken.

Bonnet family: *Je suis tellement reconnaissante d'avoir épousé l'homme d'une famille aussi incroyable. Merci de m'avoir acceptée de tout cœur dans votre famille, de m'avoir montré de l'amour et de la gentillesse, et d'avoir partagé votre fils/frère avec moi. Merci d'être la famille qui a fait de Romain l'homme et le mari, beau et protecteur qu'il est. Je vous aime.*

(I am so grateful to have married into such an incredible family. Thank you for accepting me wholeheartedly into your family, showing me love and kindness, and for sharing your son/brother with me. Thank you for being the family that molded Romain into the strong, beautiful, and protective man and husband that he is. I love you all.)

And now for my closest friends . . .

Jason, thank you, for so many reasons. You are such a loyal and loving friend, a wonderful doggy daddy, and the biggest inspiration for me to keep reaching for the stars. Thank you for always believing in me, for pushing me, for helping with Austin when I needed a male perspective, and for always being there to give me that special one-of-a-kind, calming hug that no one else can offer. I love you.

Amanza: Bestie, where do I even start? We have been through it all together, literally! A twenty-plus-year friendship like this is rare, and I truly would be lost without you. I love you, respect you, and admire your fearless take on life, and your loyalty to the people you love. You make my world more colorful with your creativity, life more fun with your humor, and you make me feel safe and loved by always being my "bodyguard" whenever I just need to take a breath from the craziness. Thank you for getting me, thank you for loving me, thank you for being one of my closest friends . . . for better and for worse.

A special tribute to my late ex-husband. You will only read this from the heavens, but I cannot leave you out. You changed my life many years ago. I was blessed to know you, learn from you, grow intellectually from listening to your brilliant mind, and to have the opportunity to love and be loved by you. You taught me, by example, how to selflessly help others at all costs, as you always did. You were an angel on earth to so many and left us too soon. You live on in my memory and are present every day when I think of others before myself. You are missed, loved, and appreciated. Forever, thank you.

Emily: A special thanks to my ghostwriter, who was essential in writing this book. You helped me safely open up to tell my story, in hopes of inspiring others. You allowed me to laugh at the funny moments and the craziness of my life and cry through the traumatic parts that I had to relive in order to put them on paper. You were so patient when I rambled and got sidetracked when my ADHD reared its ugly head during our book meetings. LOL. You are amazing, Emily. Thank you for making this book a reality for me and my readers.

Also, a huge thank-you to my amazing powerhouse agent, Jane Dystel, who saw the potential in me and my story. And my deepest gratitude to everyone at HarperCollins, specifically Lisa Sharkey, who has championed this book from day one and offered the wisest insights. Thank you, as well, to my editor, Maddie Pillari—you helped shape this book every step of the way.

To my publicist, Trixie, thank you for always protecting me and for helping me launch this book and getting it into as many hands as possible.

Finally, I wouldn't be where I am today without Adam DiVello, the creator of *Selling Sunset*, and the Done and Done Productions team, or without Netflix and our devoted fans. I know how lucky I am.

IN MEMORY OF NIKO

Photo credit: Phillip Graybill

Throughout life's ups and downs, moving to different cities and countries, through failed relationships, traumatic events, and finally epic wins and exciting moments, you were always there licking my tears away and right by my side when we got to celebrate our wins together. I'm so grateful that you made it to such an old age and got to be a part of this new chapter with me, living life to its fullest, where success and happiness were all around us. Especially when Jason, your forever papa, decided to share custody with me and become your dad. No dog has ever been more loved and appreciated than you.

You lived such an accomplished life, earning the title of Director of "Pup-lick Relations" at The Oppenheim Group, and became the first canine star of *Selling Sunset*, touching millions of hearts around the world.

Our family and friends learned so much from you, Niko, so thank you. You opened our eyes to the depths that love can reach, taught us a higher level of patience and selflessness, and showed us what true loyalty and devotion look like. You were a patient, protective, and devoted brother to your sister, Zelda, and your brother, Thor. Even at the very end when your body and mind were failing and beyond exhausted, you still tirelessly struggled to hold on for us, refusing to give in. It was our turn to be selfless and strong for you. Tearing our own hearts out so we could help you to avoid suffering was the only loving option, but the hardest thing your papa Jason and I have ever done.

We love and miss you so much already, but you're at peace now, my love. We know you are still with us, just in a different form. You live in the grass beneath our feet, the blue sky above, and the sun that kisses our skin. I struggle to find the words to describe my feelings for you, and no letter can contain the love and joy that fill our hearts, where you will always remain.

Until I make it to where you are, I'm sending all of my love and prayers to you, my sweet angel.

Photo credit: Phillip Graybill

Photo credit: Lindy Lin

ABOUT THE AUTHOR

Named as one of *Variety*'s 40 Most Powerful Women on Reality TV, Mary Bonnet is most notably recognized for her role on Netflix's Emmy-nominated, Critics Choice award–winning, and MTV award–winning hit series *Selling Sunset*. As vice president at The Oppenheim Group, Mary is a prominent figure in the world of luxury real estate and has established herself as a top-tier agent in the competitive Los Angeles market, with total sales of +$140M to date. Her contributions to the agency's success are undeniable, cementing her status as one of the leading real estate agents in Los Angeles. Beyond her professional achievements, Mary's dynamic personality, as well as her honesty and integrity, captivates audiences worldwide, and has earned her a loyal fan base. She has garnered attention and praise as an advocate for female empowerment and stops at nothing to support her team of successful women. As a self-made mogul, Mary has not always had the glitzy, glamorous life in the Hollywood Hills that we see on TV, and it shows in her work ethic, her empathy toward others, and her charisma. She currently lives in LA with her husband, Romain Bonnet, whom she married on season two of *Selling Sunset*, along with their two fur babies: Zelda and the newest family canine addition, Thor. In addition to her passion for real estate, Mary loves art and traveling.